knoc… girl

Knockabout Girl is Pip Newling's first non-fiction book. In 1999, *The Reunion*, a short film that she wrote and directed, won awards both in Australia and overseas. In 1991, Les Murray crowned her the Bard of Bellingen.

Pip has studied writing at both UTS (Sydney) and RMIT (Melbourne) and gives thanks every day for Varuna and Peter Bishop.

knockabout girl

PIP NEWLING

FOURTH ESTATE • *London*, *New York*, *Sydney* and *Auckland*

This project has been assisted by the Australian Government through the Australia Council, its arts funding and advisory body.

Fourth Estate
An imprint of HarperCollins*Publishers*

First published in Australia in 2007
by HarperCollins*Publishers* Pty Limited
ABN 36 009 913 517
www.harpercollins.com.au

HarperCollins*Publishers*
25 Ryde Road, Pymble, Sydney, NSW 2073, Australia
31 View Road, Glenfield, Auckland 10, New Zealand
77–85 Fulham Palace Road, London, W6 8JB, United Kingdom
2 Bloor Street East, 20th floor, Toronto, Ontario M4W 1A8, Canada
10 East 53rd Street, New York NY 10022, USA

National Library of Australia Cataloguing-in-Publication data:

Newling, Pip (Phillipa), 1967– .
Knockabout girl: a memoir.
ISBN 13: 978 0 7322 8326 1.
ISBN 10: 0 7322 8326 4.
1. Newling, Pip (Phillipa). 2. Bartenders –
Western Australia – Halls Creek – Biography.
I. Title.
641.874092

Front cover images reproduced by permission Australian Picture Library (Girl in car 42-15218106); Getty Images (Dirt Road to Gosse Bluff AXI:71823222); Photolibrary (Horse riders CORBIS1-00013391-001). Back cover images reproduced by permission Getty Images (Bar at Tatts Hotel NLM:10157809; Photolibrary (Cowboy RS-00000645-001); Shutterstock (Tree 1149664, Rodeo 1033539)
Cover and internal design by Natalie Winter
Typeset in Minion 11.5/16 by Kirby Jones
Printed and bound in Australia by Griffin Press on 70gsm Bulky Ivory White

6 5 4 3 2 07 08 09 10

In memory of
John
and for all those old men who have bought me
more beers than I've bought them

ACKNOWLEDGEMENTS

Knockabout Girl was initially encouraged out of me by Margaret Cameron, who thought these stories were worth hearing. The manuscript was one of the Varuna/HarperCollins Fellowship winners in 2004 and many thanks and much gratitude must go to Peter Bishop from Varuna for his early and continual support.

Stephanie Smith and Linda Funnell were crucial to the development of the book and the rest of the HarperCollins team — Julia Stiles, Mary Rennie, my editor, and Denise O'Dea, who all deserve much more than a mere 'thank you' — saw it through to the end. Thank you.

I would also like to thank Wazza and Gaz for the title.

I couldn't have done it without my agent, the fabulous Fran Moore, and friends Sarah J. Attfield, Jude Bowler and Andy Muir, who provided support and advice and lived through the writing.

AUTHOR'S NOTE

The stories you will read in this book have been written primarily from memory and many years after the fact. Everything within these pages is true in essence, polished by how I experienced it and as I remember it. I have changed the names of most of the people and have, more often than not, further disguised them. The chronology of some events has been played with to assist the reader in following my journey.

I read once that a good self-portrait reveals a depth of self-knowledge which speaks of a wider grasp of human nature. I hope what you read in the following pages paints a portrait full of contradiction and compassion.

CONTENTS

GLOSSARY

APLO:	Aboriginal Police Liaison Officer
Boat wine:	riesling from a cardboard cask; it had a picture of a woman in a boat on it, hence the name
brumbies:	wild horses
bullcatcher:	a cut-down four-wheel-drive jeep used for mustering buffalo
Emu:	can of Emu bitter beer, Western Australian brand
XXXX:	can of beer, Queensland brand
gadiya:	white person (commonly used in the East Kimberley)
gammin':	pretending; exaggerating; joking
goey:	slang for amphetamines
green can:	can of Victoria Bitter beer
Jaru and Kija:	the two local languages in Halls Creek

knockabout girl:	a female, usually young, who is up for adventure and can hold her own
language:	used when a person is speaking in an indigenous language
nulla-nulla:	piece of wood similar to a baseball bat
outstation:	a camp established so Aboriginal people could return to live on traditional lands
split the blanket:	divorce; separation
staffie:	knock-off drink for workers in a pub
stock route:	traditional route across Crown Land for moving stock
town/transit camp:	designated area for Aboriginal people to camp and stay at on the outskirts of Mataranka

PROLOGUE

At 23 years old I was looking for experience, adventure, change. I didn't have a career, a life mapped out. I had finished a university degree but now what? Sydney was proving dull and uneventful after yet another relationship had taken a dive, and many of my friends were leaving for Europe and the USA. London, Paris, New York.

I had little money and just wanted out. First it was Melbourne, then Perth for a few weeks. And then Halls Creek. Perhaps I wound up there due to boredom. And stayed because once I arrived I forgot I could leave. I thought that this could be my life. That this was where I was destined to remain — in a land of hushed desperation, of broken-down cowboys and fringe dwellers, of sunburned noses and squinting eyes, of fists and firearms. A land of dry humour born of the earth.

Water finds its level, you can't bend it, twist it, force it. You can't really make it do what you want. It meanders, trickles, seeps its way to where it will. That is how I felt living in the desert: to me it seemed everything happened for a reason even if that reason may never be revealed. A time and a place for everything. And it wasn't quite that I had no control but it wasn't quite control I was after. I was going for the real, the experience, the education.

Growing up in a small country town that I always wanted to leave meant that the old 'grass is greener over there' feeling had been with me forever. And, through books, I had developed early on a sense of the imaginary and of the big world outside the door. Of out there, over there. Of somewhere not here.

The country I went to has borders, a history, a language — all unknown to me and in many respects unknowable. It terrified and delighted, fascinated and frightened, and it stayed with me, lurking behind my eyes.

Now that I have written all these stories down I feel as though I know less than when I started. Less than that young blonde chick who swaggered into the bar did. These stories, figments of my imagination. Not real. Not now. Distant. In a time and place long, long ago. But as I write these words I feel my eyes sting and the release is palpable and I realise, acknowledge, that they all live on.

HALLS CREEK

WELCOME

Forty-four hours on a bus, in the same State, and everything I thought I had known about Australia had been stripped away. Forty-four hours of stopping at roadhouses, paying for bore water and seeing all the passengers, well all but the five of us still on the bus, leave at various places I had barely even heard of — Lancelin, Geraldton, Carnarvon, Karratha, Port Hedland, Broome.

It was the start of May 1990, just into autumn, or 'the dry' as I would come to know it, and the land was cooling. Outside the bus window the scrubby roadside grass, the red hills in the distance, the straight strip of bitumen rolled on for hours and hours and hours. For some this might have meant nothing to look at, nothing to see, just keep moving. But to me, this was the edge of the desert, the edge of Australia, where the sun sets over the sea. For this young New South Wales rural girl, this was untravelled, unseen territory.

From Broome we turned inland.

Two jackeroos, late 30s, with hard, cracked bare feet, and their swags and saddles; two young girls straight out of high school in Perth and off to work on a station outside Fitzroy Crossing; and me, a blonde (dyed) 23-year-old most recently from Sydney and, I thought, a bit wiser to the ways of wily older men.

They hadn't asked where I was going until the bus dropped off some passengers at Derby and no one else got on. Then there were five.

'You're still with us, hey. Off to Fitzroy as well, eh?'

'Hellhole,' said the other.

'You won't want to stay, but Roger, Roger here will be coming back through tomorrow. Girls, don't do any unpacking tonight. Hey, Rog, what time do you go through tomorrow? These girls want to know.'

Both men guffawed and leaned around their seats to look at the bus driver. Roger was smiling, an old joke apparently. The eighteen-year-olds obligingly giggled and looked terrified.

I knew the two men were having us on. It couldn't be that bad. Really. 'Nah. I'm going to Halls Creek.'

There was silence. Roger looked in his rear-vision mirror; the two men stared at me.

'Halls Creek, huh. What are you doing there?'

'Working in the pub.' Nervous now. How bad could it be?

'Where you from?'

'Sydney.'

Silence again. Just the sound of the wheels on the road and the engine drawing us along inexorably.

'Well, Rog, you've definitely got a passenger tomorrow.'

I smiled calmly and looked out the window. They're full of shit, I told myself.

The eighteen-year-olds now felt superior in their decision of Fitzroy. It took the men a while to reignite their swaggering repartee.

An hour later we pulled into Fitzroy.

The bus stopped at a small box-like construction with the sign 'ROADHOUSE' — though there wasn't much else to confuse it with. From where I was standing, the town consisted of a couple of demountable buildings, offices probably, and a petrol station. A short distance from the roadhouse there was a big gum tree with some older Aboriginal people sitting in the shade escaping the midday sun. Another small group, a tight little cluster trailed by small children skipping, was making its way to the roadhouse.

I could feel the heat and the red flatness of the land and the unbroken blue of the sky stretch achingly out around me, almost to the horizon. Nothing else stirred in the glare of the sun. The only sound was the slap of the roadhouse's flyscreen door as the jackeroos came out with bottles of water. Nothing. There was nothing here.

'Fuck,' I thought, 'what was Halls Creek?'

I sipped my coffee, the watered-down, instant coffee with the now familiar metallic bore-water aftertaste, as I watched Roger help the girls with their gear. A ute was waiting for them, and with a farewell glance to the jackeroos, the girls climbed in and disappeared up the highway. The jackeroos waved to me as they set their swags down outside the roadhouse. 'You take care now,' said one as I got back on the bus.

'How long to Halls Creek?' I asked Roger.

'About three hours.'

I sat back down and closed my eyes. Adventure. Anonymity. A new landscape. Distance. What else had I wanted when I left Sydney? Sydney — where was that again?

'Here you are then,' said Roger. We had pulled into Halls Creek and stopped at the petrol station. There were kerbs, I noticed as I got out of the bus. Streets with kerbs must mean something. And houses with trees, grass, flowerpots, and shops — okay, a roadhouse and a couple of tourist places that doubled as newsagent/post office/hairdresser/clothes shop. But signs. Street signs, shop signs.

'Doesn't look too bad,' I said to Roger.

'See how you go, Blondie. I come through here every day, going north or south, turn about. Just remember you can always leave. Not like some of them.'

'Thanks, Roger.'

He helped me with my bag. A tall blond white man who looked about my age beckoned me over. 'You Pip? I'm Darren.' I went to shake his hand but he had leaned down to pick up my bag. He walked to the back of a white ute, parked a short distance away, and threw it in the back. We clambered in.

'Welcome to Halls Creek. There are three rules to working in the pub. If you break any of them we will sack you without discussion.' He was staring out through the windshield, not looking, not even glancing at me. 'You are not allowed to enter the public bar of the hotel. At all. Never. You are not allowed to walk around town at night. At all. Never.' Disbelief was slowly registering. 'You are not allowed to have a relationship with a blackfella. At all. Never.' There was quiet as the heat of the day entered the cab and made my skin prickle with sweat.

Or was that my hackles rising? Even alarm bells ringing? I didn't like this man at all.

'Welcome to Halls Creek indeed,' I said.

We rode the rest of the two-minute drive in silence. It took me the first day to break the first rule, a week to break the second and a couple of months to finish the list off.

FIRST IMPRESSIONS #1

The town, as Roger had warned, was small; it had its origins back in the gold rush days of the early 1900s when Old Halls Creek, fourteen kilometres south-east of the present town, was booming with people, business and gold. When the cattle industry took over, with huge tracts of land parcelled up to create stations, the town had moved. It now sits between the wetter north Kimberley and the start of the Tanami Desert. Teeming with water north and unforgiving dry south.

Red dust was everywhere, skirting the houses, staining clothes, cloaking the kids as they jiggled along in groups. And those ordinary signs of life, the kerbs, the flowerpots, the grass, that I had used as reassurance, only extended to the first two streets of the town, the 'business district'.

I wandered about the town all afternoon, smiling at people who didn't smile back, breathing in the dry air and marvelling at the purpling hills as I made my way back to the hotel just before dusk.

The hotel itself was at the unsealed dusty red end of a street leading down from the highway. It had all-star accommodation (except for four or five), an à la carte restaurant with a cocktail bar, kidney-shaped pool with bar attached, a saloon bar and public bar. The reception and office sat between the cocktail bar/restaurant/pool side and the saloon bar/public bar side — almost a median strip between the locals and the tourists.

I met Sunny my very first night. She said, 'Hey, Pip, welcome to the weird and wonderful Kimberley Hotel. If anyone gives you shit — take no prisoners.'

I had to laugh — such a breath of fresh air after the ute. She had been in Halls Creek working as a waitress in the hotel's restaurant for a week or so when I turned up. Both of us new. Although my first shift wasn't till nine o'clock the next morning I was wondering what I had let myself in for, so it was comforting to find someone who seemed normal. Sunny had to deal with busloads of elderly tourists for breakfast and lunch and I had to deal with the drunks. Pretty even Steven really and plenty of ammunition for gossip.

She was a force to be reckoned with. A brown, vivacious blonde-streaked, short-skirt wearing, Gold Coast surfer girl the same age and with a similar sense of humour to me. And Sunny was fun — she laughed, she sang, she danced, she flirted. Her spirit welled up, overflowed and could not be beaten down. The town put us in the same category — a challenge. But Sunny was braver than me. Less contrived. Didn't need an audience, was just herself. Me, full of bravado, full of front, I had to have an audience to feel I could do justice to a story, a one-liner, a joke, a put-down. Droll cynicism was my technique, whereas unending enthusiasm was Sunny's. Loved everyone. Everyone loved her. Passionate. Ribald. Hysterically funny. Me, I was the warm-up act. The self-conscious sidekick. The second string.

MEANT TO BE BROKEN

The first day of a new job is always a test. Breakfast at eight was a quiet affair. A Tuesday morning and not too many people around. I got the keys for the saloon and public bars from the duty manager, 'Call-Me-Alex', a man with little neck, wide shoulders and dark, watchful beady eyes. As I made my way downstairs from the office to the bars Call-Me-Alex shouted after me that he would come down to show me around. It took me a moment to realise that he was pushing this remark into sexual innuendo. Great.

I opened the roller-door shutters on the L-shaped counter of the saloon bar and dust lifted in the daylight that streamed across the concrete-floored, corrugated-iron-roofed box. The opposite side of the room, where the entrance was, was open to the elements with a wooden railing along it. I would soon learn that this was where people perched to see over the crowd, although management always asked them to move. Inside the saloon bar there were a few round tables with orange plastic chairs, a row of bar stools and two pool tables, one with a slope. On the wall to my left was the jukebox.

A side entrance to my right and off the main part of the room led to the toilets and to the storage area for the alcohol. If you followed the path round the back of the toilets you came to the dog pen. The pub was guarded by dogs at night — Rum and Coke were Alsatians; a third dog died from a bait not long after my arrival. You were always alerted to the presence of the dogs because they would start snarling and barking at you the instant they smelt or heard you coming.

I turned to my left and walked the length of the stainless-steel bench, which formed the counter, past the wall with the jukebox, which separated the saloon bar from the public bar. Boy howdy. I hadn't seen that before. Between me and the customers' side of the public bar, running the full length of the stainless-steel bench, was a barricade of hurricane fencing. It had a small rectangular opening just wide enough to fit through two cartons of beer flat, or a couple of casks of wine on their sides.

And when I write the words 'public bar' — don't misunderstand me. That was its official title. The room itself was a lean-to extension to the saloon bar — just four walls with a door on the left which was the entrance for the 'public'. The 'public' being all Aboriginal. There was no glass in the windows, and the only things in the room were an old pool table, with no cues or balls, and a dust-stained jukebox which sat opposite the entry, back-to-back with the one on the other side of the wall in the saloon bar. The floor was concrete and dirty with years of use. We called it the 'front bar'.

At the end of the serving area was a narrow door into the drinking area. It had eight bolts on it, which locked from my side. They ran up the length of the door, some so high I could barely reach them. This was the door to the public bar I had been warned not to open under any circumstances.

On this first day the doors of the front bar were already open and I caught a glimpse of the red dirt, and the tables coated with a red hue, through the entrance. There was a noise outside in the front garden (not that there was really a garden, just red dirt and two picnic tables with benches, bolted and concreted into the ground) — someone was out there. Guess they would have to wait. The bars didn't open till nine.

I began cleaning, setting up the bar, stocking fridges, checking the spirits. There was that noise again. It sounded like someone vomiting. I thought I had better check. To do this, however, would be to break the first rule — don't enter the front bar. I stopped for a moment.

'Hey, who's out there? You all right?' I shouted through the gap in the wire cage. No response. 'Hey, you all right?'

A mumble came back, followed by the sound of someone struggling to stand and stagger towards the door. A young Aboriginal guy stood and swayed in the doorway. 'Hey, sis. Just wanna drink. You gotta drink for me, missus?'

'We don't open till nine, mate. And how old are you anyway?'

'Me sixteen, missus. That's all right, eh.'

'No, matey. That's not all right. I can't serve you. And you look pretty gone already. Why don't you just sit in the sun till you feel better and then get off home.'

'I need a drink, missus.'

'Well, not from me — sorry, but I can't.'

He shook his head and I turned back to setting up.

Within seconds, though, I heard him stumble towards the bar. He had a two-dollar coin in his hand and tapped it on the stainless-steel bar. 'Missus. Boat wine. Pleeuse.'

I turned back to him. 'Nah, mate. I can't. You're too young for me to serve you.'

I was just wondering if perhaps I would be asked by management to serve anyone with money, regardless of circumstance, when the boy threw up all over the bar. It was a violent hurl of red and yellow — who knows what he had been drinking — which spread across the narrow bar and dripped onto my side. It ran along the length of the bar like a sea of lumpy custard, spilling over onto the concrete floor on the punters' side.

'Bloody hell. Are you okay? Maybe I should get a doctor?' Having no idea of how to get a doctor in this town. The boy sank very gracefully to the ground. Shit.

I unlocked the eight bolts that kept the door between the serving and the drinking areas separate. Breaking the first rule. I pulled the boy to his feet, walked him outside and sat him at a table with his head between his legs. 'I'll just get you some water, mate.' I went back inside and grabbed him a glass of water. 'Now you have to sit here until you finish this whole glass. Don't move.' He managed a moan.

I went back into the bar. Mixing some metho with hot water, I sluiced the vomit onto the floor of the public bar. Then, I found a hose outside and hosed down the entire floor, washing away the vomit in swirls of red mud which disappeared instantly into the dry earth. I had just finished the bottle of metho on another wash-down when Call-Me-Alex turned up.

'What the fuck are you doing with that door open?'

I pointed outside. 'Maybe you could get this guy up to the hospital or something. He's just thrown up all over the bar and I'm sure his stomach's rotting.'

Alex looked out at the boy. 'Hey, Mick. Whatcha doing? Had a bit of a night last night, hey?' Mick turned his head. 'He'll be fine, Blondie.' Alex said. Roger, the bus driver, had obviously radioed ahead with my new nickname — and boy did it stick. 'Just leave him. But what about the door? Why didn't you call me — don't you know the rules?'

I glanced at him. 'Well, Alex, I just thought I would save you from the revolting task of cleaning up Mick here's vile vomit. You should be thanking me.'

Call-Me-Alex cracked a grin. 'Thanks, mate. But if you ever open this door again —'

'Yes, I know — you will take great pleasure in firing me.'

Mick was trying to stand up. 'Hey, missus, what about boat wine?'

I looked at Alex, who was slamming the bolts shut again. 'Nah, Mick, you're too young. You're sixteen. You need to be eighteen before I can serve you a drink.' Call-Me-Alex and I were watching each other intently.

'Mick. I never knew you were sixteen. The lady's right, mate. No more drinks,' Call-Me-Alex shouted over his shoulder as he moved past me to the cash register in the saloon bar.

As Mick sat outside sobering up and groaning, Call-Me-Alex showed me the money. Usual stuff. Till, float, change and the metho bucket. Metho bucket? 'Yeah, Blondie. All the money you get over the bar goes in the metho bucket before you do anything with it. Just give them change from the till but don't put the money in the till until it has soaked well and truly.' And why? I had never heard of anything so weird and anally retentive.

'Hep A and B. Flu, herpes, warts, anything really.'

'You've got to be joking.' No.

'Highest rate of STDs in this town.'

'Yeah, but I'm not having sex with the money.'

Call-Me-Alex laughed. 'Just do it, city girl. And you wait till some old girl pulls out her five dollars from her Namatjira handbag — you'll be soaking your own hands for longer than that money.'

I sighed. 'And what exactly is a Namatjira handbag?'

'Well, you know the painter …?'

'Yes,' I said, attempting condescension.

'Well, it's just the slang given to bras out here.'

Right. So women carry money in their bras. Aboriginal women, off the desert with no purses, carry their important bits of paper in their bras and I will want to soak their money in metho when they hand it to me because it will be filthy. Right. Now I had it. I shook my head and decided not to say anything else.

'Wait and see, mate,' said Call-Me-Alex, bumping my hip as he squeezed past. 'Wait and see.'

I felt as though I needed a bath after his body had brushed mine, let alone a five-dollar note, but by the end of my shift that day I knew exactly what he meant. From then on I gladly soaked anything that was handed to me. Money came out of crotches, underarms, bras, knickers, knots in shirts, boots (with no socks) and mouths.

THE START OF SOMETHING

I was working days for my first couple of shifts so I had nights off. This meant that since I couldn't go anywhere after dark, I was stuck in the hotel. My second night, after I had knocked off and had a shower, I headed back to the staff kitchen, behind the restaurant, to see what was for dinner. I said hello to a few people on the way, a couple of the admin staff and the housekeepers, and basically that was my evening. The chef's sausages, boiled vegetables and cheese mash were going to be the highlight. My evening, or so I thought, over by seven o'clock.

Sunny had come in and out of the staff kitchen as she was serving the evening meal in the restaurant. 'How's it going?' I asked.

'Well, I should be asking you that question really, but tonight we have 50 retirees from New South Wales — and a couple of stupid teachers who wouldn't know if they were eating hen or fish eggs.' And then she was gone.

The restaurant door swung open again. 'See you at the bar about nine-thirty. Do you drink tequila?'

'Absolutely.' And that really was that. Our friendship was sealed.

Later, as I waited for Sunny in the bar, Lea, the girl who worked nights when I worked days, filled me in on the basics. She had been in town a year, her boyfriend was Elvis, the part-time duty manager and a local, and she had respect. She took no nonsense and she gave none. Elvis wasn't quite the same, he liked a good time and a joke a bit too much to be completely straightforward, so Lea said, but still it worked. They were going to get married and were talking of babies. She didn't mention Elvis was black, something I only realised when he walked into the bar after he had knocked off.

That night, in the bar that would become my second home, Sunny introduced me to Sarah and Jim. Saviours both. They were young and in love. Sarah was beautiful. Straight backed, blonde hair, olive skin, thin and dry humoured, with a mouth that naturally curved up. Pretending to be much tougher than she really was.

Jim was handsome, tall, thin, an excellent cattle and horse man. Loved the work, the country, the people. Had time for some Aboriginal people but not for all. Flashes of temper but was old enough to pick his fights. Loved Sarah above and beyond anything else in his world. Sarah had come to Halls Creek as the partner of a concrete contractor and had met Jim. That was it. It was love. They had been in town for two years now. Jim worked on a couple of different stations, drenching stock, and Sarah did the books for their fledgling company.

Later Simon came in. Simon, who lived up in Wyndham, was a good mate of Jim's. He worked for the APB, the Agricultural Protection Board, testing cattle for TB as a job but painted landscapes because he had to. His art was beautiful. Painted by someone with an unsentimental eye. Someone with the full knowledge of the world he lived in. The layers. He was a reserved and considerate man with whip-sharp humour and the ability to underplay any moment.

He was famous for his pink singlet. The only man who could get away with not being hassled in the bar for wearing pink.

Jim, Sarah, Simon, Sunny and I became firm friends very quickly and with an intensity born out of remote places. We all laughed and drank and kicked around together. They cooked Sunny and me dinner, drove us places, offered support, gossiped, gave us background, knew everyone.

And that first night in the saloon bar set the pace and the scene for the coming months. Tourists hovering on the edges of the drinking crowd, locals (black and white), regulars (the electricians, building contractors, pilots, both fixed-wing and helicopters, Department of Agriculture officers, prospectors, roadwork crews — who used the hotel as their base in the Kimberley) and the bar flies. The humour ran high, with put-downs rampant. Gossip and insider knowledge. Who was what and who did who.

Jim said that the three of them were the few who had 'the full perspective', had the whole picture. Understood the town.

That night, Sunny was christened The Kid (as in the Sundance Kid) and me, well, Blondie was sticking. At least they hadn't thought of Butch.

THE SENTIMENTAL BLOKE

One of the daily regulars was Harry. He would come in every afternoon after finishing his day of work, building houses for Aboriginal communities.

Harry was a Shakespeare-spouting, wild man of the desert. When I first met him he announced to the whole bar that I was a leftie city chick who wouldn't last a day. I pointed out I already had. 'And smart to boot,' he declaimed to the whole bar. 'You are a sight for sore ears and eyes.'

Then he started testing me on my knowledge of Shakespeare's sonnets. Declared me an uneducated moron. Bought me a drink. Said I'd do.

'Do for what?' I had to ask.

'Peanuts and lollies said the boy upstairs.'

'CJ Dennis,' I half laughed, half screamed.

'Not bad. Not bad. And who do you think has the best legs in the place, huh?' Did I laugh or hit him? 'No one in here, that's for sure,' he bellowed. 'All the gins are next door.'

Harry had, right from that first moment, pissed me off. He was short and fat with a beer belly that was as tight as a drum. His hair was long, his beard was straggly, he had two front teeth missing and he had a penchant for rum and Aboriginal women. He was smart and funny and told incredibly misogynist jokes. He was so crude that he made cowboys blush, and that's saying something. I took to calling him The Sentimental Bloke after his knack of pulling quotes from CJ Dennis in answer to questions.

Harry lived with a black woman, always had some said, but often insulted Aboriginal people in general. Proudly said he had kids all over Western Australia but never gave his exes (white or black) money or support for them. Worked hard and actively disliked anyone he thought was lazy or a malingerer. Quoted Shakespeare perfectly and knew the Bible backwards, had been to a private school in Perth, but wound up running wild in the desert for most of his adult life. Well educated but full of crudities and put-downs. Was canny and sly and knew how to manipulate people. He hated the police but often drank with them and would stand up beside them in any fight. Loved black women, spoke warmly of his lovers, but would also talk of 'black velvet'. Despised anyone who called him a 'gin jockey'. Was completely trustworthy but would get himself so pissed he couldn't walk.

And he always knew what was happening in the outside world. The world beyond the small town dramas and bullshit. The world outside of Halls Creek.

And then there was the day he stepped up and king-hit someone who had been hassling me for hours across the bar. Harry got to the bar about 3 pm and by 5 pm the guy, who hadn't let up all afternoon ('Hey, girl, you seeing anyone?'; 'Who do you see in your break, honey? You wanna break me?'; 'I've got the time, blue eyes'), was pushing my patience. There is something incredibly grating about an arsehole using terms of endearment. After two hours of hearing this guy go on at me, Harry made him stand up and simply swung at him. The guy was on the ground before anyone knew what happened. I bought Harry a beer and forgave many, but not all, mind you, of his sins.

So, soon after meeting him, whenever I went anywhere, driving to Wyndham, flying to Alice, mustering in the middle of nowhere, Harry knew. It was comforting in a way, knowing that someone would start the alarm if I didn't turn up by the appointed hour. He confounded and delighted me. I adored him.

FIGHTING TIMES

There wasn't much to do in town except hang out at the hotel. While there was a motel with a bar just a couple of streets away, it was never as popular or as busy as the bars at the pub. Everyone, at some stage or other, ended up in one of the bars.

The hotel was the breeding ground for gossip, the place to kick start an affair, to hear the results of the shire elections and to know who was wanted by the police and for what. The townspeople and tourists displayed their loyalties, fears, anger, jealousies and joy, all well lubricated with alcohol.

Fights were commonplace. Black on black, white on white — they were manageable. Lea, who had worked the saloon bar for a year now, taught me very quickly that the easiest thing to do was to buy the fighters a beer each and ask them to take it outside. They usually went. Whatever happened off pub property was not our concern apparently. The police rarely did anything about stopping a fight outside the pub unless there was a separate reason for them to intervene.

And if there was a fight on or the pub was too busy to manage and we needed to distract the crowd for a short time, Lea or I would lean over and get one of the guys to put Yothu Yindi on the front bar jukebox and either Hunters and Collectors or Midnight Oil on for the saloon bar. 'Yolngu Woman' was the front bar favourite, followed closely by the Warumpi Band's 'Blackfella/Whitefella'. 'Throw Your Arms Around Me' or 'US Forces' did the trick for the saloon bar. People would all sing along and dance and a sense of fun would be reinstated. At least until they got their next drink. Music does have an immediate and extraordinary power.

White on black fights or black on white — they were different. Always nasty and always escalated very quickly. The front bar, where the drinkers were all Aboriginal, went off if a fight started between the colours, even if only over a spilt beer. They would try to get into the saloon bar, reach through the mesh, hands trying to squeeze through impossibly small holes or run out the front entrance of the hotel in an attempt to get through the main entrance. The police, who were always present from early afternoon, usually stopped most of them at the gate.

As soon as a fight got really out of hand, Lea and I, both short, would leap up onto the bar top and pull down the roller door shutters on both sides of the saloon bar. We would have to be as quick as possible as the most likely outcome of a pub brawl, once it got going, was that one or two of the blokes would try to jump the bar and steal a carton of beer or bottle of spirits or seven. If we were unlucky, we would cop some kind of projectile while we stood on the bar, high above the punters, fully exposed.

The shutters would slam down as we jumped to the ground on the inside of the bar in time with their descent, lock them and tell the front bar drinkers to shut up. Lea would pick up the nulla-nulla which was always under the counter, I would mix us a drink or grab two cans, and in the sudden bubble of safety we had created we would have a quick sip. Then we would duck out through the tiny square of an exit into the storeroom, locking that door behind us, out the storeroom door, locking that, and then stand on the side of the bar watching the fight. Really we should have sold tickets.

KEEPING THEM KEEN

In the kerbless part of town, where the majority of Aboriginal people lived with dusty front yards and pots of flowers struggling in the dry, dogs roamed everywhere. All kinds, all sizes, all ages. I had never really appreciated the expression 'mongrel dog' until I saw some of these dogs. Not crossbreeds, not bitzas, not half-breeds. Mongrels. Long legs with square heads and short bodies, stumpy tails, brown spots on white and black stringy coats, scruffy ears and yellow teeth. Even the small terrier dogs, and the cute toy dogs, who were meant to be held and patted, snapped and bit and played rough.

In the *gadiya* area of town, near the shops and closer to the pub, the dogs were kept inside fences and gates. They were healthier, shinier, pure breeds. Alsatians, heelers, Labradors, kelpies and a red setter. Well-trained, well-fed, well-loved, but all these dogs barked at Aboriginal people whenever they walked past — and that happened every ten minutes. The odd thing was, though, that when I went to visit my *gadiya* friends their well-trained guard dogs didn't bark at me. I could never figure this out.

I wondered about it out loud during dinner one night. Fish, a forty-something cynical cattleman, had turned up with some fresh steaks and invited us to join Jim and Sarah at their house. Fish was the target of much of Sunny's energy and the invite seemed to her to be a breakthrough in relations, so off we went.

It was only the third time Sunny and I had been out of the pub at night. A rare treat. Jim and Sarah's place, a square two bedroom weatherboard house, was on the main thoroughfare from one side of town to the other. This meant that lots of Aboriginal people, the only people who walked anywhere at night in Halls Creek, walked past all night. This meant dinner was accompanied by regular barking from Samson, Sarah's two-year-old Alsatian, and was then followed by a chorus of other fenced-in dogs further down the street.

'Why only black people? Why doesn't Samson bark at everyone?' I asked.

Jim, a known practical joker, just said 'We trained him.'

'Why train him just to bark at black people?' I paused to think about this. 'And how? I mean dogs are smart but that smart?'

Jim and Fish passed a look between them. 'Well, most of the shit that goes down around here is by blackfellas so you want your dog to warn them off. And if you get them when they're puppies, it's easy. You put the cute little things in a hessian bag, tie off the end so the pup's in total blackness, and then rough them up a bit.'

I wasn't quite sure what Jim meant.

'You put them in the bag, tie it off and then you pick up the bag and drop it, kick it, roll it over a bit. The pup gets real scared. After a few minutes of that you get a blackfella to open the bag.' Fish and Jim were starting to laugh. 'Yeah, for twenty bucks, or even ten if you're lucky, the poor black bastard opens the bag. That cute little thing, who isn't so cute any more, sees the blackfella and goes for him. Forever after, the dog hates blackfellas. Really useful round here.'

The table was watching me.

'But that's awful,' I said.

'Yeah, yeah, Blondie. Doesn't hurt either of them. And it is useful. Although I did once see a staffie pup go for a blackfella and really do some damage.'

On the way home, as Sunny and I walked the five minutes back to the hotel — one of our first night-time ventures by foot and still a real novelty, this time as a result of an argument win with Jim about whether he was too pissed to drive us — I wondered about the barrel-like blue heeler that always went for whites. His owner was a black man. The dog's name was Smart.

JEAN-PAUL DE HALLS CREEK

Jean-Paul was a hairdresser and makeup artist. I don't think I ever asked him when he came to Halls Creek or where he was actually from. His accent was exotic enough to answer all my questions: Paris, France. He was well known and most people respected him, even if they did talk behind his back or, in some cases, to his face.

He was also the only hairdresser in Halls Creek who would cut Aboriginal people's hair. There was another 'salon' that only *gadiyas* went to, but I, and those residents who had any sense of style, went to Jean-Paul. He knew how to cut hair.

The Aboriginal kids would pile into the back of the shop where Jean-Paul had his basins and chairs. They would chatter and fidget waiting their turn. All sent by their mothers. And yes, there were infestations of lice, and lots of unwashed, filthy hair. But Jean-Paul would cut it all. And without comment, apart from, '*Mon Dieu*, daaahlink, if I don't, who in this town would?'

Jean-Paul would also keep tabs on the kids. There were always kids on the streets of Halls Creek. And they were mostly black kids. Except for a few tearaways, the white kids were kept off the streets. Bundled into cars or yelled at to 'Hurry up.' Especially the girls. But there were always black kids at the town basketball courts and hanging around the shops. Jean-Paul's shop. The roadhouse. Kicking around the post office. Waiting. Watching. If Jean-Paul saw them on the street when they should have been at school he would always stop and ask them what they were doing. Then he would relay the information to their mothers, aunties or sisters. As he often said, 'If they get to school today, it is a good day, daahlink' with a wave of his hand and a flick of his fingers, full of 'it's no trouble!'

He and I used to drink cocktails in the pool bar when I wasn't working. As we watched the sun disappear from the sky and the sunbakers wrap up against the desert chill, we'd pretend we were somewhere else — anywhere else — and we would talk fashion and love and life. Green creamy grasshoppers were his favourite drink. He christened himself Jean-Paul de Halls Creek. Thank you — daahlink. And it really suited him. Such flourish and flamboyance was rarely seen in the desert and he was like a cool breeze from the south on a stifling day — unusual, disarming and someone you will always remember.

While we sat sharing cocktails, Jean-Paul had told the story of when he had first heard of Australia and Aboriginal people. He had been young, a teenager, and he had read a story in the French version of *National Geographic*. The article detailed the journey of a man who was dying from cancer. He had come to

Australia and lived out in the desert with a group of Aboriginal people. Over some months the medicines and treatments they gave him cured his cancer — or at least sent it into remission.

After reading that article Jean-Paul had always wanted to live out here. He found Halls Creek and that was it. He'd lived here ever since. Fitted in and became a local. Perhaps he was welcomed because he was so completely unusual. Or perhaps it was because Jean-Paul thought Australia, '*Mon Dieu*,' the people, the colours, the animals, everything about the place, was amazing.

I thought Jean-Paul was amazing.

TWO-FISTED LOVER

Weapons were always an issue. Not so much guns, although there were lots of them; mainly fighting weapons: knives, broken bottles, bits of wood, pool cues, pool balls, glasses, cans, chairs, tables, cutlery — whatever they could get their hands on in a rage. Or even just for fun.

And not only men either. Women were just as bad. Sometimes worse. And not only black. Don't imagine for a second that the white men and women didn't fight just as much. And dirty. The whites fought dirty. Always reaching for anything to use. Not trusting their hands. Smashing beer bottles. Squashing cans. Breaking pool cues.

One of the most mesmerising fights that I ever witnessed was between two Aboriginal women. One older, one younger. Both a bit pissed, with beanies lopsided on their black curls. They'd been in the front bar for a couple of hours and gradually their conversation grew more heated. And then they were off.

The younger one slapped the older one. The older one threw her glass of boat wine in the younger one's face and stormed out the front entrance onto the red dirt. The younger one chased her and started beating her on the back. The older one turned and smashed her fist into the other's face. The younger one stumbled back and the older one kept walking away.

The younger one ran after her and threw herself on the older woman's back. They both hit the ground. Dust flew up and hung in the morning air around the two of them. The older one seemed really angry now. She wrestled the younger one off her and lunged for a star picket, one of the heavy triangular metal fencing posts which had been used to protect some long-dead seedling.

She wrenched it out of the ground and turned on the younger woman. The younger woman took a step back. 'Hey, sis,' I heard her say. The older woman stepped towards her and said something in Jaru that I couldn't understand. I was growing anxious. Even though the women were off pub property and this fight was no concern of ours, it felt that at any minute it was going to get ugly.

The younger woman lunged for the other star picket that had been guarding the seedling and there was a clash of metal. 'Shit.' On the one hand I was fascinated by the two women facing off. Like warriors. Samurais. On the other, those star pickets could really do some damage.

I yelled out to Call-Me-Alex and kept up my 'Hey, girls, come on. Nah. Stop,' but I certainly wasn't going to get much closer to the two of them. There was another ring of metal on metal and angry words screamed at the top of their voices. Of course the news had flown around town and now a sizeable crowd of enthusiastic bystanders had formed. Of no practical help whatsoever, they just chipped in with words of advice for the fighters. Quite bipartisan.

Call-Me-Alex turned up. 'Blondie, aren't you meant to be behind the bar?'

'I wanted to check these girls don't kill each other.'

'It isn't our problem, Pip.' There was a pause as we both watched the circling combatants. 'But it's a good one, hey.'

I turned to look at him. 'Fucking hell. Do you think you could call the cops then?'

He just smiled and kept watching. 'Shit. I reckon they're going to draw blood.'

'Fuck.' I ran back to the bar and called the cops.

The police turned up in a paddy wagon, two officers and a whole crowd of people streaming down behind them. And then the cops just watched. One even sat on the bonnet of his car so he could get a better view.

The clash and ringing of metal was becoming rhythmical, and I guess kind of reassuring because they hadn't actually hit each other's bodies.

They must have been getting tired though. The fight had been going a good fifteen minutes already. The younger woman stumbled. The crowd took a collective intake of breath as we watched the arc of the older woman's picket. It landed squarely on the other's torso, with a dull, fleshy, sickening thump. The younger woman hit the ground and rolled over, moaning. The older woman swung again. This time landing a blow on the younger woman's legs, splitting one open. The blood didn't seem to flow, just flesh peeled back to the bone.

The crowd quietened and a couple of people made to move towards the women, but the older one stopped and rested her star picket on the ground. As she leaned against the picket she spoke in Jaru.

The younger woman, who wasn't crying or even visibly in pain, stood up, albeit with some difficulty, said something in reply and they hugged. I suggested to the cops they take the younger woman to the hospital, a short drive up the road. The younger woman shook them off. Both women headed back into the pub. The older one, cheeky as ever, yelled at me to hurry up. 'Miss, two boat wine, Miss Blondie.' So I headed back to the bar. They drank. They laughed. And then they went off to the hospital.

All over a man. The older woman's husband. She won the fight so all was right with the world.

MOVING TARGETS

The first time I saw a sawn-off shotgun was during one of the busiest nights in Halls Creek. It was a hometown AFL football weekend. A Friday night. Both bars were going off, jukeboxes loud and only Lea and I on. On nights like this we could easily take $10,000. It meant we had to run. And watch the crowds closely.

I was serving the jammed and drunk front bar. I turned with three plastic cups of boat wine for a customer and there, level with my face, was a shotgun. Its long barrels cut off, dismembered, pushed through a gap in the mesh. Pointed at me.

'Right. What would you like?' I had no phone. I couldn't see any security. And I didn't want to get shot. The guy holding the gun smiled. 'Hey, Blondie. Just beer. Green cans. Cartons.'

'Okay. I'll just get them for you. I'm just going to reach down and get you some, okay.' I didn't want him to think I was doing anything else.

Risking a glance at Lea who was too busy to notice, I reached down to the fridge behind me with the Victoria Bitter cartons in it. The rest of the packed front bar was continuing to party. But some punters were lining up to watch and maybe to grab one of the cartons as they came out.

I pulled out a slab, pushed it through the serving gap in the mesh and swung down for another one. The first one was passed out through the bar and then the second. Fifteen in all. And the whole time that stumpy, ugly piece of grey metal was pointing at me.

'That's fine, missus. That'll do.' The guy smiled, his white teeth shining. 'Thanks, Blondie.' And then he was gone. Through the crowd. Out the front.

I screamed to Lea, for one of the bar managers, but it was too late. The beer was gone. The guy was gone. The sawn-off was gone. And no one knew anything. They just wanted more drinks.

For some reason I came across quite a few truckies who enjoyed the feel of a sawn-off. Perhaps it was their loner status. They weren't usually from the desert, they were from long distances away. Passing through and finding comfort only in the familiarity and sameness of bars and hotel rooms. Tired people. Pressured people. Always worrying about their schedule. And always on some kind of amphetamine. Something to keep them up. Keep them going. Keep them positive. Always with some kind of confidence booster.

Or perhaps it was that their road trains were so awe-inspiring. The kick and rush of the dust and engine. The grinding gears. The smell of the cattle in the back or the petrol in the air. The horn blaring. The way they bore down on you even if you pulled off the road and stopped. That moment when you looked out your window and watched them speed past, only centimetres away from your face. The anxiety building and then flooding away. And the trail of dust left for you to follow. Maybe the truckies needed to add to their own sense of superiority, in competition with their vehicles, with the unpredictability of a sawn-off.

One morning a truckie rocked in to the saloon bar about eleven. He'd parked his rig out the front. White goods. Delivery from Perth to Darwin. He was speeding, on amphetamines when he came in. Clearly been awake for too long but not going to be close to sleep for hours. He started drinking.

It was a busy day. Tourists most of the morning. Locals most of the afternoon. A band was playing that night. Lots of people coming and going. Every now and then the truckie would check his watch and mutter, 'Still okay. Still on time.' He kept drinking and disappearing into the bathroom for top-ups of his cheap goey (which he had also been selling in the bar). He certainly didn't look like he should be driving anywhere that night.

Just before the band started, I guess about eight, he finished his drink and said he was off. Staggered out of the bar and disappeared into the dark.

It must have only been five minutes before he was back. Waving a sawn-off and screaming. 'Which one of you lazy fuckers did it? Who took my stuff? You fucking mongrels!' Everyone dived to the ground. Lea and I telepathically told each other it was too dangerous to jump up and pull the bar shutters down. Shit. Lea was nearest the phone and reached up for it. She dialled the cops, and then the restaurant, to get some help down here. Where were those bullshit brave bar managers when you needed them?

The truckie just kept on yelling. And then he fired into the ceiling. People scattered. Hiding behind tables. Trying to run while they were crouched to the ground. The shots stuck hard into the corrugated iron — or went straight through — and luckily didn't ricochet off anything.

The silence after a gunshot is penetrating. The intense and detailed quiet that only fear can bring. The bar waited. Then the truckie started yelling again. 'Who's got it? Where is it?' Lea and I slowly sneaked a look over the counter. Two cops were coming down the path behind the guy, with their guns out.

'Hey, mate,' said one. 'What's going on here?' The cop sounded remarkably calm. 'What's happened?'

The truckie turned around on his heel. 'They stole my stuff. They took it out of my truck. All of it.' He had lowered the gun so it was aimed at the ground.

'Right. Well you better show us where it happened. Is that your rig out the front?' It was one of the good cops, who was routinely hassled and called 'yella fella' because of his mixed Aboriginal, white and Malay heritage. But he was also called the Golden Rod because of his reputation as a lover — he had charm.

The truckie said, 'Yes, it's my rig and it's fucking empty. It was full of white goods when I parked it there this morning. Now it's fucking empty. Fucking niggers.' The shotgun waved around in space.

'Right. We'd better have a look then. You want to show us?' The cop stepped sideways and indicated that the truckie should lead them out the front. As the guy passed them on the path the two cops jumped him and had him on the ground, unarmed, within seconds.

The truckie was arrested for carrying an illegal weapon. He didn't have a gun licence either, and they charged him with armed hold-up as well. Serious. His rig spent two days out the front before the trucking company organised a pick-up driver. No one was found with stolen white goods — not officially anyway. There were a couple of families whose clothes suddenly seemed cleaner. I still wish I had seen the line of people it would have needed to lug the dishwashers and washing machines through town and into homes …

NOTHING COMPARES TO YOU

Helicopter pilots up there were like cowboys of the air. My first experience of them was Pete and Kim. Pete older, having just turned 30, and Kim my age. They mustered cattle throughout the winter. Operated out of a huge cattle station in the Northern Territory and were based in Halls Creek for a mustering job for the duration of the dry or until there were no more animals left to muster.

Pete was sexy in that Marlboro Man style. Kim was taller, strapping, but he inhabited his space in an unformed way, tall and gangly without the angles, almost lumpy. With their caps, boots, jeans and swagger they really looked the part. And just like cowboys of the land, they partied hard, drank hard, worked hard and ate lots of meat. Added to this they were both single, so every girl, white or black, in town was after them. The saloon bar was suddenly filled with girls in way too much makeup and very short skirts.

Pete was a smooth talker and happy to be seen as available. Not necessarily going to do anything about it but certainly keen to talk and flirt. Kim was different. He was more likely to make dumb remarks, drink too much too quickly, and flirt self-consciously. So self-consciously that he often walked away from a conversation without finishing it, midsentence. Embarrassed. And he would watch the room. All the people in it. Us behind the bar. The cops. He could tell you what was going to go down before it did. He was very useful on busy nights.

The two of them were at ease with each other. They enjoyed their work, couldn't imagine doing anything else ever, and they enjoyed each other's company. They were mates, and you wouldn't want to pick a fight with one because you would have to take on the pair of them. I once saw them fight back to back for a solid half an hour. And they still came out grinning.

There was, however, a transient, empty feeling to both. They relied on each other because they never stayed long in any one place. Pete had been married before. Back in Queensland. And no one really knew Kim's story but obviously he was wounded. He would drink Bundaberg Rum all night and then go to the jukebox and put Sinéad O'Connor's 'Nothing Compares to You' on repeat. Melancholia and confusion of the worst kind. But his very woundedness made him sweeter, more attractive to women.

One day Kim's helicopter was grounded, and even though he'd been sunning himself around the pool reading he looked at a loose end — not sure what to do or where to go. I'd stopped off for a chat in the morning. I saw him at lunch and we had a laugh about something inconsequential. Then I was in the saloon bar for the afternoon shift. It was midweek, pretty quiet and Kim came in about two.

'Mind if I sit here?'

I smiled. 'Nah. Two's company. And I still won't be busy if number three turns up. Beer?'

He grinned. And I mean grinned. He didn't really smile. It was either a nothing kind of open-faced listening expression or a grin. 'U betcha. And I think we need some music!'

I got his green can while he put some money in the jukebox. 'Kim, you know you don't have to do that. It's free.'

He grinned again. And shrugged. Soon there was music blaring, country followed by some pub rock.

And we settled in for the afternoon. Occasionally I would serve people, clean, restock, but really Kim and I just chatted. He read me paragraphs from the paper. We talked about cattle, mustering, flying helicopters. He promised to take me out mustering. 'I am going to hold you to that! Let's go tomorrow!' He enjoyed my straightforward enthusiasm for risk and excitement.

The Joker, an Aboriginal man with a belly as round and hard as a basketball and a wild afro to complement his check shirt, blue jeans and Cuban-heeled boots, was also the town's pool shark. He came in looking for a game. He and Kim started to play. Kim had been a tough kid, in trouble with the cops whenever he had been in a town, and the adage about 'misspent youth' was true in his case — he knew how to play pool. It was great spectator sport, watching two good, evenly matched pool players take each other on.

Often The Joker wouldn't play to his best so he could scam the tourists (you know the one about letting them win a game and then raising the stakes so he could beat the pants off them), but this afternoon the bar was really quiet so The Joker was cutting loose. All the while Kim kept drinking, switching from beer to rum.

Gradually, as the light changed and evening arrived, the bar filled and I knocked off for the night. Kim wanted me to sit with him but I begged off till I had had a shower. 'Come over to the pool bar and wait for me, I'll only be a minute.' So he struggled up and we walked through the hotel reception, past the cocktail bar, then out into the night air, the brilliant mass of starlight still visible even with the lights of the pool bar on.

Of course, this walk was enough to get people talking. Gaye, who was doing the cleaning rosters as we walked past reception, was instantly jealous and her usual sour demeanour turned venomous as the gossip flew. Kim crashed on a lounge chair in the open while I went and got changed.

When I came back, he had fallen asleep but the air was getting cold, really too cold to be out without a coat. I nudged him and he stirred. 'Kim, come on. Wake up, matey.'

He sat up and leaned back against the lounge. 'You the romantic type, Pip?' he asked.

I laughed. 'Yes. Absolutely.'

'Then sit alongside me and keep me warm.'

I leaned into him and wrapped my arms around him. 'You're pretty cold, Kim.' He nestled in closer and said nothing. And my body relaxed in his hug; being held was something of a dim memory for us both. We soon fell asleep.

In the middle of the night I woke up with a start. Some of the staff were going back to their rooms after closing the restaurant and they had made some noise passing us. As I stirred, so did Kim. The position we had been curled up in wasn't great for spines. Both of us stood up, stretching, and looked at the vast array of stars. He started to tell me a story.

A story of how, when he'd been a boy, out in the middle of the desert with only cattle and a couple of black stockmen for company, he had heard the earth sing. He described the desert quiet and the stamping of the cattle's hooves and how he had never felt scared, even with all the inky blackness enveloping him.

We stood away from the arc of artificial light falling around the hotel, and the stars seemed to lower, as if we could have reached up and touched them. His voice was lifting and rolling as he explained the way the ground had swelled under his feet and he had felt the earth sigh. Of the rhythmic breathing of the warm dirt and how he had felt every cell in his body release. He had stood between the air and the earth, different but not separate from either. And then he had heard a humming, building into a honey-coated rumble with perfect pitch and regular, languorous intakes of breath. It was then, he said, that he knew he was going to fly. To catch the updraught and hover in a middle ground, just above and below, in between the sky and the earth. His helicopter was now the only place he really felt at home.

The stars were so close and the horizon so black that it was as though we were wrapped in a blanket. And then he started to weep.

I realised that whatever it was that was making him shake with sobs, not many people knew his version.

We stood together in a shared silence, watching the night. Eventually I said, 'Hey, Kim, if you do want to tell someone I can be a good listener.'

My voice seemed to waken him and he gently kissed me on the forehead. Then he turned and we both looked back at the hotel. He sighed. 'I really do think I should just go bush and that'd be it.'

'Yeah, but you'd have to hit town for rum!' I said softly.

'No, I reckon I'd organise a drop-off. Get someone to leave a case every so often at the corner of a bend somewhere out there and I would never have to see anyone ever again.'

I pulled him closer and squeezed him. 'Yeah. But where's the fun in that?' We slowly headed back to the bar, blinded by the electric lights.

Even though something had been revealed the night before, I wasn't expecting any marked change in Kim's behaviour the next day. Of course, he was embarrassed. He didn't really talk to me. Talked to everyone else, including all the females he came across. Best he could do for me was a 'Morning, Pip' and a shy grin, followed by a blush because word had spread.

'Hey, Kim. How you doing?'

So far every man and his dog had commented on my 'lucky night'. The whole town knew. Jean-Paul was sympathetic — except he couldn't figure out why nothing had happened. 'I think, Jean-Paul,' I replied, 'because Kim and I are friends. Not lovers, and I don't think I want to be his lover.'

Jean-Paul said something about not being dumb enough. And I had to ask him to repeat it. He lifted his head up from washing a regular's hair. 'You're too smart, Pip. They want you for talking, not loving. They only want the dumbies to fuck — you they want for dinner.'

I was pretty sure it was a compliment, especially with that French accent, but I would have to think about it.

As I went back through the hotel to my room I literally bumped into Kim and Gaye coming around a corner. 'Hey, how's it going?' I said as I walked past them. Kim looked deeply embarrassed. See, I thought, I haven't even done anything and still the one-upmanship of small-minded, bored people is inescapable. I did have to smile though — Gaye was looking every inch the cleaner she was employed to be. Watch it, Pip — karma will come full circle.

ANSWERING PRAYERS

The autumn days were still hot so it was a sweaty drive. The white vinyl seats stuck to our bare legs. The road, both in front and behind, was a strip of dust. The heat from the engine made the future shimmer and wave, and I couldn't help wondering what we must have looked like from a helicopter. An old bright purple Holden station wagon winding its lonely way through the Kimberley Desert. We hadn't seen another vehicle in hours.

Sunny and I had borrowed Matt's car. Matt was a signwriter, hence the purple and the word *Signwriter* and his phone number down each side of the car. Sunny and I had driven out to the nearest waterhole — 200 kilometres away or thereabouts. There hadn't been much water in it but we had had a dip, a beer and some lunch. It was just good to be out of town. It was still sunbathing weather during the day, if you were out of the wind.

The sun was beginning to set in front of us. Pinks and oranges burning up the sky, as the shadows lengthened and the mountain range turned to indigo. The air was growing thick and it was almost as if we were in some kind of dream — everything felt slow and timeless. Breathtaking and breath-giving at the same time.

We rounded a bend and I saw, up ahead, a truck, a one-tonne with a cage back, stopped on our side of the road.

I began to slow down and two nuns came round to the back of the truck to wave us down. Their white habits looked surreal. Starchy, pure, untouched amongst all the red dust. Apart from their knees.

'Maybe they've been praying,' said Sunny.

'And look what they've got in reply.'

I turned to Sunny as I stopped the car. 'Have you ever changed a tyre, Sun?'

'No,' she giggled, 'you?'

I was trying really hard not to laugh at the absurdity of this. 'No. But I've seen them do it in movies all the time. I'm sure we're up to it.'

We got out of the wagon and said 'Hi' to the nuns. 'Been here long?' The nuns seemed speechless. Perhaps they were disappointed in God's response. One of them grabbed my hand and pulled me over to the back right-hand wheel. They hadn't even been able to get the jack in properly.

Sunny and I started at our God-given task. We got the jack in. Then we got the wheel off. That only took 30 minutes. We were filthy. Covered in wet red, streaky dust, sweaty and hot, even in the cooling air. In the back of the nuns' truck, in the cage, was a huge pile of tyres, all in various states of roadworthiness. 'At least they came prepared,' Sunny whispered. The nuns had still not said anything to us and I could hardly stifle my laughter at the absurdity of it. We had both been trying so hard not to take the piss but things were getting out of hand. We chose a tyre from the back which we thought would be okay. It didn't seem flat (we kicked it) and it wasn't bald.

The nuns in their glaring white, both tiny even compared to my five foot one inch, just watched. No expression passed across their faces. I felt as though we were completing some kind of test — maybe we had died and gone to heaven but St Peter was off for the afternoon and these nuns were restructuring the entrance exam.

As we began to pump the tyre up with their whizzbang foot pump, the nuns crept closer. The foot pump meant Sunny didn't have to expend much energy and the tyre appeared to be inflating. We then heard the faintest of 'hissses'. 'Fuck,' I muttered. As the tyre sighed flat, the nuns looked at us as if we were the most ridiculous people they had ever come across.

Sunny and I were both now tired, sore and filthy. We had already been at it for an hour and a half. We unscrewed the nuts and rolled the flat tyre off. Sunny went back into the cage and started to hunt for a better tyre. She threw three onto the road just as the second car we had seen all day careened past us, dodging the tyres and almost collecting one of the nuns. The guys in the car screamed at us and kept right on driving. The dust they left behind made me finally understand that expression 'eat my dirt'.

One of the three tyres Sunny had picked out stayed pumped up. We kicked it a few times just for good measure, and to redeem ourselves in the eyes of the nuns.

We finally got it on and everything packed away. We turned from the back of the cage as Sunny locked it, to say farewell, but the nuns were already in the cab, gunning the engine and … gone. One of them stuck her hand out the window — in thanks? 'FUCK!' screamed Sunny. Ridiculous. Hilarious. I laughed till I cried. We were filthy, late, and for the second time that day we had to spit out mouthfuls of red.

The pinks and oranges were gone. The country had deepened to a blue black and I had to use the headlights all the way home.

CONFESSION

With June came winter. The night chill off the desert took much longer to leave the mornings, and the afternoons were full of bone-warming sun, cut by dust-lifting breezes and too-early shadows heralding another cold night.

He had first come in on a quiet afternoon. He sat at the bar by himself, deep in thought, a wiry, greying nugget of a man. He started on beer and after a third moved to Scotch. I didn't realise he was a Father, a man of the cloth.

I finally got around to asking him where he was from.

'Out on the desert.'

'Where?'

'Around. Between here, Balgo and Warmun.'

I had flown to Alice one weekend; we had stopped at Balgo to pick up a couple of passengers and Warmun was Turkey Creek, the other side of town towards Kununurra. I had some idea of the distance he meant. 'How long you been up here?'

'Eight years.'

'Out there?'

He nodded.

I poured him his second Scotch.

'How about you? I haven't seen you in here before.'

'Sydney. Decided to see Australia.'

'Well, here it is,' he laughingly said.

He asked where I had grown up.

'Nowra.'

His eyes brightened. 'Oh really? You would know the big church. The Anglican one. By the river. Big old thing with the neon cross.'

'Yes. I always thought it seemed so straight-backed, full of self-importance. The way the neon could be seen from all over town. Watching. Judging.'

He didn't respond.

'What about the church?'

'Oh, I filled in for the minister there. For a few months.'

'How long ago?'

'About fifteen years I should think. That minister. What was his name?' He was watching me to see if I was going to retrieve the name.

'Michaels! Yes.'

He smiled. 'Michaels. Did you know the family?'

'Well, I think one of their daughters went through school with one of my sisters … But no, not really. I know who you mean though.' He stopped talking. Seemed as though that second Scotch had sent him over.

A couple of guys came into the bar. Aboriginal men. The older one had scars and he didn't speak or look at me. 'Hey, Father,' said the other. 'We're going. Gotta go now.'

Father turned and smiled. 'Surely. Yes. I've been having a lovely chat with this young girl.'

I flashed a smile at the guys; I knew the younger one, Eric, who got all shy and diffident.

'What's your name, lass?'

'Pip.'

'Lovely. Breath of fresh air. Gotta go. See you next time then.' He picked up his hat and attempted to stand up.

'Yes, Father, see you soon.'

The two men giggled and helped Father up. Yes. That second Scotch had done the trick.

Father turned back to the bar, stopping the guys in their tracks and the three of them stumbled. 'Funny, isn't it,' he said, looking me straight in the eyes. 'Funny how years pass, distance is covered and your past turns up, fresh as a daisy?' He nodded and they left.

The bar grew still, calm, but calm with expectation, the quiet before a storm. I felt as though I had just heard confession.

Father usually only came into town every six or so weeks, which was why I had been working at the pub for a while but we hadn't met. Two weeks later he came in again, something which became a talking point around the pub. He sat at the bar and I worked behind it and we chatted. We talked about my uncle, also an Anglican minister, who had been up to Fitzroy Crossing and around abouts when I was a child. Of course Father knew him. Liked him. Even though we both declared 'irascible' was the word to describe Uncle Greg.

By June the region had erupted in AFL madness. Each weekend the pub was teeming with people because there were three matches on. Everyone was in town. The population literally grew by thousands on weekends like this. Good thing really because the cold desert wind whipped through the open bar, but when it was full of people no one really noticed.

Father came into the saloon bar on Sunday night — his visits were fortnightly now, regular as clockwork — and asked for a Scotch straight up. He looked bad. Sick and tired and worn around the edges. Frail but somehow stringy, lean. Drier. He sat in the corner near the jukebox all night. Watching people drink, fight, play pool, dance and drunkenly romance. The winning team came in and some white bastard said he would buy a round for them. Of course, every person to a man, woman and underage baby wanted one and they clamoured and clambered up to the bar. I caught Father laughing sourly at the bar full of tanked-up people screaming for more.

We shut early that night. The coppers turned up in the bar an hour before closing. They'd been breaking up fights all weekend and were sick of it. Slowly people finished their drinks and left for wherever they were sleeping that night. Relatively smooth really. The cops only hurt one guy, black; as they threw him out of the bar onto the concrete path, they missed the gap. Father was still there in the corner. The police were about to ask him to leave as well but I shook my head. 'Hey, Father, you can sit there while we clean up. No hurry.'

The cops helped themselves to their knock-off drink (as they always did, even though they were still technically on duty) and wanted some gossip. Lea volunteered to take the money up to the office to count it — I had to talk to the cops. We talked about the teams, the games, the fights and the next weekend.

Father was included in the conversation and occasionally reacted with something that resembled laughter. 'You know,' he said in one lull in the conversation, 'I've always wondered about you blokes,' looking at the two cops. 'I mean, why do you do it? They're all going to be back tomorrow. What's the point?'

The coppers were taken aback and instantly defensive. 'Well,' said one, 'if we weren't here, all hell would break loose.'

'Mate,' said Father, 'tonight was hell.'

The cops had no idea how to respond or what he meant. I had to smirk.

'Do you believe in a humanity?' Father asked, and then with a wave of his blotchy hand continued, 'Well, regardless, you saw it tonight in all its fucking God-given glory.'

The other cop, the one we called Ugly due to his abusive tongue, his leering manner and his general aggression, decided to take offence. 'Mate, watch it, all right. We do our jobs. And that's it. We don't judge anyone. If they break the law they're ours. Simple as that.'

'What about you, Pip? What do you believe in?'

Father's question panicked me. 'I guess, I guess, the freedom to live how you want to live so long as you aren't hurting anyone.'

Father nodded. 'And that gets you through the night, does it?' His flippancy stung and registered in my face. There was silence as I grasped for words. 'Oh fuck it,' he said. 'You're probably too young to have nights of interminable, clawing wakefulness.' He almost spat the words out of his mouth.

By this stage the cops had decided he was just another drunk and not worth listening to. 'Come on, mate. You staying here tonight? We'll get you back to your room.'

Father shook them off. He seemed more like a boxer, albeit a shrunken, grey-haired boxer, than a minister and I could see where this was leading. 'He's okay, guys. I'll get him home. Leave him be.' They looked at me and though we all knew they wanted an excuse to take him, they nodded and left with their guns, fat arses and shit-brown uniforms, locking the gate after them. Funny how the cops had keys to everything in this town.

Father smiled. 'Sorry, Pip, but those bastards bore me stupid.'

'Are you really okay, Father? Really?'

He looked at me. 'No, not really.' He sighed, the Scotch-driven melancholy reasserting itself. 'I don't know what I'm doing here. I don't know what you, or any of us for that matter, are doing here — or what the Church is doing here.'

The silence of the empty bar wrapped around us. I poured us both another Scotch.

'You've been up here a while now, Father — probably too long to keep your sanity, especially out on the desert without a proper home, and this town, this town is a mad place. Couldn't you go away? Maybe a holiday back down south?'

There was another slow pause. The day had been long and noisy, everything was slowing down around us.

'Don't know where I'd go.'

'Where's your family? Where's home?'

He drank some more Scotch. 'See, Pip,' with sarcasm creeping into his voice, 'maybe you'll get to the point in your life where you know what you have done, you can see the choices you made years before and see how every little piece of your life has led to this moment. As if all there is is fate, a prescribed destiny.' The sounds of the night desert were seeping into the bar. Dogs calling, retreating voices, thumps and bumps, and the sound of distance, of a landscape that moved on outwards from this bar, this moment.

'You say that, Father, as though you don't believe in a God that guides you through life.'

'Don't believe in any God, Pip.' And there it was. Out in the opening hanging between us in the silence.

I had no idea what to say. I was hardly the person to try to argue for a God. I just looked at him. Mortified, knowing his lack of faith was too huge to comfort.

'You see, Pip,' he said after finishing his Scotch, 'when I think of home, it's not a place, not even people. It's just her. Her embrace and the way she used to look at me. That's home.'

I waited to see if he was going to keep going. 'Where is she?'

'Nowra. She's that minister's wife.'

The earth seemed to take a breath and sigh. But that might have just been me.

Gradually he told me the story. Of how he and Michaels had first met at theology college. Of how Michaels' fianceé had become a friend. The three of them, all caught up in youthful Anglican fervour. Then later they remained friends, although not in close proximity. Years passed and Michaels became ill. Wound up in hospital just after taking on the Nowra parish. So Father went down there. To run the church and the parish while Michaels recuperated. And the wife and he had an affair. A passionate white flame of an affair. Never any question of anything else.

But now, years later again, here he sat. Bereft, except for a memory of a feeling, of a safe haven, of a home within an embrace. The sheer magnitude of his emptiness, of his barren interior, wiped out all attempts to comfort. I got him to his room and made sure he set his alarm because he had to get a lift early the next morning back to his camp. And then, as was my normal practice, I had a bath to wash the grime of the bar, of the day, off my skin. It was after three in the morning by the time I got to bed. I lay awake until dawn wondering about life. The human condition, the desire to belong that humbled us all.

Father called me Tuesday night. Odd, I thought, but really he just wanted to thank me and to let me know he was safe.

Friday morning I was opening the bar. Nine o'clock. I always found opening relaxing. It wasn't busy and the quiet was meditative. I could think my own thoughts right to their end.

Call-Me-Alex came in. 'Hey, Blondie.' His beady eyes squinted at me.

'What is it?' He wouldn't normally show himself before eleven and he seemed hesitant. I stopped wiping down the tables and turned to face him.

'You knew Father, didn't you?'

I looked at his small head and over-cultivated neck muscles. Past tense. There was a slight pause as I heard something shatter, or splinter, or fall away into air.

Call-Me-Alex leaned towards me. He was trying to decide whether he should touch me. He stopped midway to reaching my arm, his arm hovering in space.

'They found him hanging. They think he did it a couple of days ago. The police went out to his camp early this morning.'

His hand finally reached mine and he touched it for a moment. 'Let me know if you need a break.' And he turned and left the bar.

LANCE AND THE TURKEY SHOOT

Old Lance had been up in the Kimberley for 40 or so years. He was employed as the gardener for the hotel. He would wander about in his khaki shorts and buttoned shirt — always pressed — attending to the gardens and minor handyman jobs. He was leathery and brown with a sock-mark tan at his ankles and a deep frown inscribed in his forehead. Not an easy laugher. For whatever sins I committed in my past lives, older men, like Father, like Harry, confided in me, and Lance was no different. He took a liking to me straightaway.

When he had finished his cleaning, gardening or fixing for the day, he would make his dinner in the staff kitchen, feed the dogs — Rum and Coke — and sit down with a bottle of rum to drink. It almost seemed to be stewing him and always made him loose-lipped, sleazy and bitter.

Lance and I would have discussions about all sorts of

things over lunch and dinner but they would more often than not end awkwardly as his right-wing, racist, homophobic and misogynist ideas came to the fore. I would carefully lead the conversation back to his colourful gossip-filled stories of previous generations of Halls Creek residents.

I remember one afternoon I was reading out by the pool. The sun was warm enough to last another half-hour or so and Lance came up for a chat. I sat up and slipped on a T-shirt — he always made me feel self-conscious — and he sat on the next lounge. I could smell the rum from two feet away. He liked baiting me and often called me a clueless city chick. He started to talk about winter in the desert in the past and asked me if I had ever heard of the turkey shoot.

'Turkeys? You mean native turkeys? Bush turkeys? Are there some up here?'

'Oh yes. Native turkeys. Not so popular nowadays but we used to go out in the night and hunt them. Really easy targets.'

'And do you still do it? Aren't they protected?'

'Well, it's not public any more. We don't tell anyone we're going, you see.' There was a curious glint in his eyes. 'You should come one night.'

'Sure. Although I'm not really up on killing living things. Especially defenceless birds.'

'Defenceless?' he smiled, 'Yeah, these don't even see you coming. But they aren't birds. Native but not birds.'

I looked at him. 'But you said turkeys.'

'Yeah, but that's just because of the noise they make as they go down. A collective jabbering.'

I was slowly getting worried. 'Lance, you aren't telling me that you shoot people, are you?'

'Nah. Course not. They aren't people, Blondie. Not like you and me, and really we're all probably better off. Especially them.'

I stared at him in shock. 'And you've been doing this for years? And everyone knows about it?'

He stopped and looked at me. 'Well, looks like I had you pegged all wrong. You really are just a city slut slumming it up here.' His face was fierce and clouded.

'Yes. You got that right. I'm slumming it with present company.'

He stood up and walked away. We never spoke again.

WARNING SIGNS

Eric, the son of one of the town's large families, and I had been eyeing each other off for quite a while. Elvis kept telling me he was trouble. Which I, of course, didn't believe and didn't quite mind if 'trouble' was what I got. Anyway, they were related in some way. Just men being boys, I thought. And word had got around. There was gossip. About Eric and me.

We didn't see each other often, he rarely came to the pub and when I saw him in town it was always with other Aboriginal men. But on the rare occasion he did come to the pub, we would sometimes touch as he was saying goodbye. Then it graduated to when we were passing in the street. He'd grab my hand quickly, his dry skin smooth like a pebble against my soft pale fingers. Always with the promise of more.

I was never sure whether the 'more' would arrive, or if he was just playing a *gadiya* girl because he could.

I saw his mum, Belle, around a bit. She and I often chatted when we ran into each other on the street. She never came to the hotel. Eric was her youngest and most wayward. Of most concern.

One afternoon, late, Eric and I ran into each other at the post office. It was getting dark and I should have been heading back to the hotel. We stopped to say hello. Slightly awkwardly. 'Why don't you come home for dinner?' Eric asked. 'Sure.'

They lived in the Aboriginal part of town — dusty, darker, poorer. We walked there. It wasn't often that I was able to walk through the quiet streets at night, listening to the desert and seeing the stars come out in the darkening sky. This night felt special. Different.

Eric was quietly spoken and charming. Genuinely interested in me and what I thought. Where I was from. My family. He grabbed my hand and his skin was warm. Welcoming and secure. We walked along the unlit strip of road that led to the basketball court. Then across the court, where some of the kids were playing, and then onto his street.

I was nervous. 'Is Belle at home? Is it okay for me to just turn up?'

He smiled. 'She'll be fine. You're with me.'

There were noises coming from the houses as we walked past. Television and conversation. Kids arguing, resisting bedtime. We reached their house. The lights were on and the front door was open.

'Hey, Mum.' Eric kissed Belle on the cheek.

'Hey, Belle. I hope this is okay. Eric asked if I wanted to come for dinner.'

Belle, always gracious, 'Of course it is. Come in. Sit down. We were just starting to eat.'

I couldn't read her to know if it really was okay.

We all sat down, Eric's sister Lou and her two small children, one a year and the other three years old, Belle, and Eric's Aunty Sally. They were lovely. I realised I was relieved. And pleased. It felt almost as though they liked me. And it had been a long time since I had wanted anyone to like me. I suddenly realised that my time in Halls Creek had been a pretty lonely period, with Sunny, Jim and Sarah my only allies.

Dinner was finished and I helped clear away the dishes. So did Eric. Belle went out to a meeting with Sally, and Lou put her two children to sleep. When she came back out we were sitting on the couch talking. She put the TV on and we began to watch a movie. But all I could think about was Eric and what his skin felt like against mine. What would it be like to kiss him? To hold him? He looked at me and smiled. Out of sight of Lou. Just for me. He was thinking the same thing. He grabbed my hand and said, 'Let's go outside.'

We sat out the back, on chairs in the red-dirt backyard. And we kissed. A delicious soft and slow kiss. Later we snuck back into the house and went to his room. The three-year-old was asleep in a cot on one side and Eric's double bed was on the other. Our investigation of each other was tender and funny. Trying to keep quiet so we didn't wake the child, while not wanting to limit ourselves. One of the funniest moments was when he pulled out two condoms. And put both on. 'What's that for? Your sperm extra strong?'

He laughed. 'You just can't be too careful.'

The morning came with a bolt of sun from the window. It was suddenly bright and day. I rolled over and saw him asleep. His face soft and calm. The three-year-old had crawled into our bed and was wedged in between us sound asleep. There was some noise in the kitchen and I realised that the rest of the house was awake. And that I was embarrassed. I stretched and edged my way out of bed. I dressed, turning to see him awake and watching me, kissed him, said I had to go, and asked him to come see me soon.

I quietly left the house without Belle or Lou seeing me. The walk back to the hotel was light and clear, or rather I felt light and clear. Something had changed. The internal delight of being touched, desired, made for a great morning.

Of course word got around. I think it probably took a couple of hours. In the afternoon Elvis came to talk to me at the bar. 'Pip, look, Eric's okay but he's trouble. Especially for women. And don't think it's serious. Okay. You don't want it to get serious. And he has other girls in other towns.'

I didn't mind. I didn't want anything specifically. It was fun. It was nice to be looked at by a good-looking guy who didn't just want to push me up against the side wall of the pub and fuck me. Elvis understood my point, my desire, he just thought I was being naïve.

A couple of days later, not having seen Eric since that morning, I ran into Belle in the supermarket. We were both there to meet the food truck. Frozen milk, semi-frozen vegetables. If you didn't get there first on delivery day, you didn't get anything vaguely fresh. She smiled at me and I thought we were okay. 'Thanks for dinner the other night. I enjoyed it.'

Belle was a smart woman. And she always had her eyes on the prize, so to speak. 'Yes. It was good. I just hope you realise that Eric is promised to a girl in Kununurra. She's expecting his baby.'

I hadn't known this and I was sure that Belle knew Eric wouldn't have told me. She was warning me off at the same time as trying to reassure me that she didn't think less of me for sleeping with her son.

'Look, Belle, I don't want to get in the middle of something. I didn't know that. You know, Eric is a great guy.'

'Who can't keep his dick to himself,' Belle put in. 'And he plays girls all the time. And I have to say *gadiya* girls. He doesn't fuck around with black girls. And you do need to be careful. His last *gadiya* girl wound up in hospital.'

I was shocked by her forthrightness. 'What happened?'

Belle sized me up. 'Pip, you're a smart girl. What are you doing up here? Huh? You come here swanning around, being the friend of everyone in town. Not being easily categorised. Not sleeping with anyone. Not taking sides. No one knows what to do with you really. And then you sleep with my son. You pick my family. Me, who most people are scared of — and for good reason.'

I was confused now. Is that what she thought of me, what the town thought of me? Was it bad?

I looked around the small supermarket. There were a couple of people obviously watching but most of the others were pretending to shop.

'What happened to his last white girlfriend?'

'He beat her up. He often beats up *gadiya* women after he has slept with them. Had a relationship with them. The last one didn't press charges. And no one in this town wants to see you beaten up. Don't see him again. Is all I am saying. Not for me or for him but for your own safety.'

I walked out of the supermarket stunned. Went and sat in Jean-Paul's for a few hours. Jean-Paul gave me whisky and a good talking-to.

'*Mon Dieu,* daahlink. Don't see him. Belle wouldn't say those things about her own son if they weren't true. You have to look after yourself. She's right though, no one in this town wants to see you beaten up.'

I went looking for Elvis when I got back to the hotel. 'Is that what you meant when you said he was trouble?'

Elvis was uncomfortable. 'Yes. That's his form. You should stay away from him.'

So I did.

NOTHING COMPARES

Nothing much had changed between Kim and I. He had got over his embarrassment as soon as his helicopter was fixed and he could disappear all day, and we'd gone back to our comfortable conversation and general good humour. And lately he and Pete had been busy, sometimes not in town for days on end, camping out on the desert near the stock or at the station, so I hadn't seen much of him at all.

A few weeks after 'that night', though, Kim was in the bar late, by himself. Pete had headed off to bed. The hierarchy of the town meant that the land-bound cowboys wouldn't really socialise with the helicopter pilots. Same with fixed wing. Fixed wing wouldn't socialise with any of them. Ever. Each group thought they were better than the others. So Kim sat by himself with his back to the railing, facing the bar but on the other side of the room, just watching me.

'Hey, Pip,' he called. I glanced up. 'You're looking beautiful tonight.'

I shook my head and smirked. 'And your rum goggles need a clean, mate.'

He stood up and swayed over to the bar. He leaned up against it with his back to the wall, wedged in between the counter and the jukebox.

'Play "Misty" for me, miss.'

I had to laugh. 'Sure, cowboy, you got a dime, I got the time,' I managed in a pretty bad Texan drawl.

He hunched over and stared down at the bar. 'You're too nice, Pip. I'd like to root you, but I think I need your friendship more than a hot night between the sheets.'

Charmed, I'm sure. 'Well everyone needs to be needed, Kim.'

'U betcha,' he slurred with his trademark grin.

The bar was pretty empty really. The cops wouldn't have much to throw out tonight. I started to clean up. Kim swung around and put some coins in the jukebox. They jangled as they hit the bottom and without looking up from the fridges I was cleaning I said, 'Kim, how many times do I have to tell you, you don't have to pay.'

'Ah,' he mumbled. 'So now you tell me you're free. Now she tells me.'

Sinéad O'Connor started singing. By now I knew every word and sang along under my breath. Kim was deep in some thought that involved skolling the dregs of his rum and smudging the ring of sticky sweet liquid his glass left behind on the bar with his fingers.

As the second verse began I stood directly in front of him. 'Kim, hey, Kim,' I said. He looked up at me. 'What's with this song?'

He shrugged. I put my hand over his on the bar and held it.

Then, after a moment, turned back to my cleaning. I didn't hear him leave the bar.

It was closing time, and I locked up, told the cops they couldn't have a staffie, and headed back to my room.

As I crossed the open stretch of ground between the pool and staff accommodation I felt someone come up behind me out of the shadows. I turned, nervous. 'Shit, Kim, don't do that. You fucking scared me half to death.' He moved closer to me and came over all cute, walking really close to me with his arm around my shoulders. His size dwarfed me.

'Shh, Pip. I could hardly wait out here for you with all those eyes and ears on the watch. I had to lurk.' I opened the outside door to the block of staff rooms. 'Have a look down the hallway, see if anyone's there,' he whispered in my ear. I leaned into the brightly lit but dingy hallway. Empty. We headed quickly to my room, one of the far ones right at the end of the hallway, and got inside without anyone seeing us.

Then I realised that Kim was in my room. I was instantly nervous. The room was pretty much just that. A bare, chipped-fibro broom-cupboard of a room. I had decorated by painting the window frames and buying a rug to cover some of the dark-brown hideousness of the carpet. And on one of the walls I had Blu-Tacked cuttings from newspapers and quotes and writing and letters and photos. Kim was transfixed by these and stood reading and touching all these scraps that had caught my imagination.

'So, do you want anything else to drink?' I asked, as I pulled out my half-empty (or was that half-full?) bottle of gin.

'So you were going to have a quiet one by yourself, hey,' he said jokingly.

'I often do, Kim. I often do.' I poured two drinks and he sat on the bed. I sat on the old lounge chair I had scrounged from one of the regulars. 'Cheers.' Our glasses clinked. I took my shoes off and put my bare feet on the bed, relaxing into the chair. He leaned back against the wall and put one hand on my ankles. The air between us wasn't hot with sexual frisson by any means, more like slipping into a favourite old coat.

There was a quiet gathering of thoughts. 'You know, Pip, it's not often round here that a girl is just friends with a bloke.'

I smiled. 'Yeah, I know. Stranger than fiction, isn't it.'

'But I like it. I like it a lot.'

'Good,' I said, suddenly feeling it, 'cause I'm not expecting anything else. I mean, hell, sex'd be great but not with you, Kimino.'

Another pause while we thought about that. 'Do you reckon bad sex is better than no sex?' I asked. 'I've often wondered what guys think of that.'

He shrugged and slyly said, 'I would say, good sex is better than bad sex but that bad sex is always better than nothing, yeah?' He was grinning now, laughing at me. 'U betcha.'

The quiet was almost conspiratorial. 'Hey, Pip, are you around next week?'

'Um, like I was going shopping in London but I can give that up to be here in Halls Creek with you. If you would prefer.'

Silence.

'I have to go back to Adelaide for the week.'

'Oh yeah? For anything in particular or just family?'

'Both really. I have to go to court. And see my family.'

'What are you going to court for?'

'I have to give evidence at an inquest.'

I was watching him closely. 'Whose?'

The room seemed to grow smaller as if it was trying to hold him close. 'My fiancée's.'

And then he told me the story. Of how she had been the prettiest girl in South Australia. How they had known each other since school. He had asked her to marry him. A big wedding planned. Loads of guests, bridesmaids, pageboys, catering, flowers, all white. Everyone was excited. A match made in heaven. And then on the morning, the morning of the wedding, he had got a phone call from her. She had driven out to her cousin's house to get ready, a little way out of Adelaide, and she wanted to see him. He reminded her it was bad luck but she didn't care. She really wanted to see him. He, in his wedding coat, got into his ute and headed off.

About twenty minutes later he swung into the drive of the house. Kim walked up the path to the door. He was a bit nervous, thought this was unexpected, but not anxious. As he opened the door and called her name, there was a gunshot. Close, just through the kitchen. He called to her and ran into the lounge room, frantically trying to figure out if someone was shooting at him. Scared for her. Momentarily forgetting what had brought him to the house.

And then he saw her. On the floor. Lying on the floor in her wedding dress. All the white satin quickly turning red, the stain spreading from her neck down. The gun still in her hand, flung out to the side of her body. Kim couldn't breathe. He stood for a moment and then ran out of the room.

The police came first. And then his mother, father and brothers. And then her mother and father. Surreal. They were all in tuxedos and floating 'after-five' dresses with strappy shoes.

Kim told the police what had happened. He had nothing else to say. His family was shocked. Everyone was appalled. The bride-to-be's mother was speechless, silently distraught. And then the police said it was his gun. Which it was, he realised. They began to ask him slightly different questions, with a slightly different emphasis. About his mood. His actions. Where was he when he heard the shot? Did he touch the gun? What time had she called him? Whose phone did she use? Was anyone else meant to be in the house with her? Slowly, even though the police kept reassuring him he wasn't a suspect and his version of events was believed, he realised they were suspicious of him. Even though there was never any doubt she fired the gun and he wasn't in the room at the time, they remained suspicious.

So, next week, he was off to court to answer questions. The same questions he had answered previously. The same questions that always left him guilty, torn apart and confused. But it was for the last time. This was it. The final step. The coroner would finally determine the cause of death and that would be it.

Kim let out a long breath. I just sat and looked at him. Not being able to imagine. I began to cry. 'Shit, Pip. You're not meant to do that. That's me.' He leaned over and hugged me. 'But I'm all right now. I'm getting better. I don't drink as much and I only play that song a few times a night these days.' There was a silence. I could feel him breathing, fast. 'I'm still pretty fucked up though.'

A strangled laugh escaped my breath. 'You are fucked up and fucking mad and now I know why.' I wiped my eyes and the silence grew. We lay down on the bed and slept, clothes on, snuggled tightly into each other.

Such a peaceful sleep is rare. I still remember the sweetness of the morning light as we both stretched into wakefulness.

We arranged to go mustering a few weeks later. We tied yet another hangover on the night before. It was a raucous, ribald evening of jokes, fights and too much rum.

The next morning at four-thirty, as I stood outside his hotel room in the receding gloom of night, shivering in the pre-dawn chill, I could hear Kim swearing and stumbling as he struggled into his clothes and boots. I had been up for ages, too excited, even with a screaming headache developing, to sleep.

We met Pete in the truck and drove the short distance down the road to the airstrip where they left their tiny mosquito-like helicopters, the ones with no doors and fibreglass bottoms. The sun was lifting in the east and in the western sky the moon was a brilliant white sliver. The motors were flicked on and any residue of peace disappeared in the hard metallic whirr. The blades spun and the air was jammed against the ground, everything covered in an instant cloud of dust.

With helmets and seatbelts on and the radios hooked up so Kim and I could speak, we lifted off the ground.

Flying south-west, the land fell away, and as I peered down at the country below, my feet, resting on the fibreglass, looked large against hills and valleys and the flat red in between. It was exhilarating. So open and windy, the sound deafening, even through a helmet with in-built earmuffs. Kim and I yelling at each other, me smiling fit to burst, him groaning mid-hangover, bemused by my enthusiasm.

Droning along the curves of the land he swept low over hilltops and down through river valleys, close enough for the water to ripple at our presence. I was yelling in excitement, repeating 'It's amazing, it's fantastic' over and over again, to the point where Kim was clearly fed up with his overexuberant passenger. He took us high, fucking high, literally straight up.

The world looks incredible from up there. The sun was glaring and bleaching the land with its harsh light; there wasn't a cloud in the sky and the horizon was impossible to keep in eyeshot. Then the engines stopped. It was immediately quiet, just the blades slicing through air with a fast whispering whip of a noise. I turned to Kim, anxious but not entirely convinced that he hadn't done this on purpose. He didn't look worried at all.

We sat in the air, maintaining our position for a good few seconds, and then the whole helicopter started to sink as the blades slowed down. My stomach lurched and I looked back down at the ground way below and then at Kim. He was watching me closely, not quite laughing, waiting to see how I would react. I momentarily kept my head and then started to yell. 'Kim, what the fuck are you doing?'

He was looking straight ahead, out the front of the helicopter, as though he was waiting for something to happen. The blades were slowing and their noise had changed to a deep *whick*. I almost panicked but it was all so quiet and beautiful that I couldn't quite convince myself that there was anything wrong. The ground began to rise up towards us very fast and I began to wonder just how far we could drop safely.

I turned to Kim and he was grinning at me. 'You look as white as a ghost, mate,' he yelled, his voice loud in the growing quiet.

I kept my eyes on his as he laughed and laughed, simultaneously flicking the switch for the engines to cut back in. Nothing happened but he was still laughing. He flicked it back down and then up again. The screech of metal working hard against metal was deafening as the blades sped up, the list we had acquired righted itself and we soared back up into the heavens.

I was screaming with fear and adrenalin, laughing with tears rolling down my face. 'CAN WE DO THAT AGAIN, KIM?' I yelled into the wind.

He shook his head with hungover amusement. 'It was meant to shut you up, Pip, not make you ask for more.'

AN EXAMPLE

He came into the bar by himself. Drank by himself most of the afternoon, even in a busy bar, played pool and won a few and lost a few. He was tall, thin, with dusty jeans, checked shirt and cowboy boots. Long, curly hair with obvious knots. He didn't quite look like he had been sleeping rough, but almost. He was clearly from the desert with his long legs and long hands and fingers, but none of the Aboriginal people in the bar really spoke to him. Most often if anyone was in town off the desert they were included actively in whatever was going on — funerals, fun, conversations in the bar. But it seemed as though this man had a space around him, an invisible aura through which no one passed.

He went to the bathroom and I had to ask. The Joker just nodded and moved away from me. Harry pretended not to hear. Elvis came in. I repeated my question.

'Yeah, Pip, I wouldn't worry about him too much.' He was

trying to avoid me and was being shy at the same time. I hadn't seen him shy before.

'Elvis, obviously he is someone. Something. Is he initiated? Or something like that?'

Elvis was now smirking. 'Some would say he is.'

The man came back from the bathroom and a path opened up for him through the crowd.

'So is he someone Aboriginal people are scared of? Cause they seem to be this afternoon.'

Elvis was watching the man walk back to his drink and sit down again. Still untouched by his surroundings.

'Sometimes it's just best if you don't know things, Pip.'

'Like secret men's business, you mean?'

Elvis sighed. 'Mate, you ask a lot of questions.'

I served more drinks. Emu, Emu, Scotch and Coke, rum.

'So where is he from? The desert?'

Elvis looked at me, suddenly tired. 'You aren't going to let this go, are you?' He shrugged. 'He was caught with a woman, not his wife. And he was punished. In some communities it's the worst sin. Especially if it's against skin. Someone he shouldn't have been with. Like a relative or something.' More drinks handed out.

'And what was the punishment? Must be something bad if everyone knows about it.'

'He was whistlecocked.' Elvis began to walk away from me.

'What's that?'

Without turning around: 'They sliced his penis in two, from tip to base. He can't even piss straight.' And he was gone.

GADIYA GIRL

It is night and I am riding my bike back from dinner at Jim and Sarah's house. It is dark, inky black and I am alone on the street. Riding in the still, cold air that stirs as I pass through it. Marvelling at the shapes of the old gum trees, black against the stars that throw no light tonight. And then I hear the quiet padding of feet behind me. I glance around with a shot of adrenalin. Two boys. About twelve years old. Skinny and grinning. Running behind me. Black and fast. They are catching up. I pedal harder but the creaking bicycle has limits. Then there are more voices. More than the two boys. A chorus of children, calling for me to stop. In any other town, in any other place, at any other time but not tonight. I speed up, standing on my pedals. There are ten or so I guess. All running, all calling, all chasing me and all nearly catching me. I don't look behind again. I just focus on staying in front and riding towards the light. The one lonely street light on this stretch that signals the corner. The corner that leads to the hotel. Nearly there. If I get round the corner there will be people. There will be the police van. There will be lights. The children are close. They are almost beside me. Enjoying the chase. I can feel their excitement. I have no idea what they would do if they caught me. Probably nothing but perhaps because of the rum I drank with dinner, I'm not going to find out. I am nearly at the corner. We all know they will disappear if I get round it. They surge behind me, all of them closer and calling underneath their breath. *Gadiya* girl. *Gadiya* girl. Stop. Stop. We want to touch you. Hey, *gadiya* girl. I am in the pool of bright white cast by the street light. I skid in a wide arc around the corner, glance back as I straighten up and find more reserves to pedal harder. They have gone. Voices burbling in the darkness outside the light. Laughter ringing underneath the trees. In front of me the hotel is lit up like a Christmas tree with the cops out lurking. I keep pedalling. A second glance behind me and it is as if nothing happened. The dust of my skid has settled. The air is still and the circle of light undisturbed. I hear my breath, my heart in my ears and feel the blood racing around my body.

LANGUAGE

Simply by working in the pub I had picked up the basic swear words and put-downs for *gadiya* people, and any female, in Jaru, one of the local indigenous languages. There were two main languages, Jaru and Kija, as Halls Creek sat on the border between these two countries. There were more people in town who spoke one of those languages, or even both, than English. So when I enrolled in Jaru classes I was a bit shocked to find that I was one of only two (white) people in town wanting to learn it.

With only two takers it was likely that the Jaru class would be cancelled. Matt, the language centre coordinator, and Will, the elder who was going to teach the class, noted that the adult education pottery class was full, as was the Thai cooking class.

'Really?' I asked. 'With whites or Aboriginal people?'

Matt threw a look of feigned disbelief to Will and then back to me. 'With the high school's teachers, actually.'

'Do they all speak Jaru?' I kept on.

Will smiled. 'Well, Pip,' he always called me by my name as opposed to Blondie, 'you would like to think so, wouldn't you.'

'But how do they teach the kids if they can't speak their language?'

Matt sighed. 'With great difficulty.'

The teachers we were talking about were usually straight out of training, from Perth, and had taken the option of working in the desert for a year or two to place them higher on the list for allocation to the schools and districts they wanted to live and work in, often back in the richer suburbs of Perth. None of them, apart from the principal and a couple of the other teachers, had family in Halls Creek or had lived there longer than a year.

The Kimberley Language Resource Centre was an amazing place. I used to go and hang out with Matt just for the sheer inspiration. The centre had been set up to preserve the languages of the Kimberley. It was always full of very old Aboriginal people sitting on the ground talking.

The inspiration came from the fact that these people, who didn't know how to speak, let alone write, English, were creating English translations of their languages.

These old people would come into the centre to learn to speak English. Then they would phonetically translate their own language into English and create an alphabet which was then taught to local indigenous children.

The old people were so keen and full of determination and joy at the idea that their languages might be spoken fluently by future generations that they came in no matter what. Every day. All day. There was a sense of urgency and support for the task that I have never seen since. Anywhere.

RUNNING AMOK

Living and working in the pub made Sunny and me feel as though we owned the place, that we belonged. We thought we were indestructible. We had few rules we paid attention to and we had no one from our past (or our future) to keep tabs on us, so when we decided to let go, we let go — no holds barred.

One of these occasions was an ordinary weekend in August. We thought about going away. Alice. Darwin. Broome. Fitzroy. All possible. But we decided to save the dollars and kick around town.

Both Sunny and I had worked day shifts on Friday. Friday night we sat in the pub. Arguing. Gossiping. Dancing. Laughing. And disturbing the pool games. The Joker, in the middle of a winning streak, nearly clobbered us because Sunny and I thought it would be completely hysterical to dance, Esther Williams style, on his pool table to 'Rock Lobster'. He got pretty annoyed but he couldn't really go us because we were white chicks, staff of the pub and had friends, who were also his friends, in the crowd.

The pair of us were forcefully assisted by Jim and Simon in our decision to leave just before closing; besides, if I wasn't working I didn't want to have to witness a closing, no matter how totalled I was.

Saturday morning was beautiful. The dawn was slow, with the sun gradually, gently revealing the desert, travelling across the distant ranges, highlighting creases in the flat stretches of red around town, and burnishing the green of the trees until they were difficult to look at next to the lapis blue of the sky.

We had bought salmon, sour cream, bread, eggs, chives and fruit, as well as a few bottles of champagne. Breakfast by the pool. Fish, Jim, Sarah and Simon all joined us. Along with Sal, the restaurant manager, a great lady from Broken Hill who had cornered the market on razor-sharp one-liners. Elvis and Lea turned up early on as well but didn't stay. Elvis always felt uncomfortable in an all-*gadiya* gathering. Especially when we were being completely self-indulgent; not that he thought we shouldn't, he said once, it was just that he didn't really know how to do it.

By one in the afternoon Sunny and I were the only ones left. Everyone else had gone off to their various days and we were plastered. But champagne plastered. Happy. Silly. Been swimming and caused havoc for one group of guests. Pulled out the water pistols and attempted to shoot the pool bar staff — while they were serving customers. Call-Me-Alex had already warned us once. His neck muscles doing overtime. Did we care? Nup. We were having fun.

We decided we needed to move location. And that meant holding up the office. With our water pistols. As police officers. Funny! God we laughed. Of course Gaye and Lindy, who were manning the phones, didn't think it was so amusing. We kept telling them that water didn't really affect fax machines. I mean, really, it wasn't that much water anyway.

We sat on the front path of the hotel in the afternoon sun. The street was a wide strip of red dirt and gravel which turned into bitumen further up towards town. It had a few trees either side but looked, and felt, flat and never-ending. At one end of the street was the hotel. At the other end was the police station. Seemed preordained really. I wondered if the police station had been built there for easy access to the hotel — the major source of its clientele.

Sunny brought out a hipflask full of Scotch and we had a swig. Purely medicinal.

'Hey, Sunny. The police station's up there.' She turned her head and looked. 'Hmmm. Wonder who's on duty?'

The idea formed in both our minds at the same time. With pistols refilled we headed off.

Sneaking into a police station in 1990 was relatively easy. And the Halls Creek station was no exception. We shushed ourselves as we went up the stairs. Sunny, doing her best impersonation of Lacey (I had to be Cagney), slowly opening the front door and leaning into the office.

We could hear the cops having a cup of tea and a chat out the back near the kitchen. There were at least two of them. One of the voices I recognised. Ugly. We decided to go for it anyway, in the name of a good laugh. We lifted our water pistols and ducked under the counter, quickly rounding the corner of the short corridor leading to the kitchen. Our sandshoes didn't make any noise but we were trying really hard not to laugh. I have never been able to figure out whether it was Sunny or I who half laughed, half choked, but a noise was made. The talking stopped and suddenly we had two policemen, a young guy from south Western Australia and Ugly himself, in our faces. Well, their guns were in our faces.

Now, although we were both pissed, Sunny and I had had enough guns pointed at us in the last few months to take them seriously, regardless of our or the gun's circumstances. We dropped our water pistols.

'Hi, guys. How you going?' I managed in the silence after the plastic hit the lino. 'We were a bit bored and thought we'd come and visit you. You know, brighten up your day.' I thought it best to keep talking.

The young guy, Lionel, lowered his gun. 'Shit, Pip. You should be bloody careful. Walking in like that. And with those.' He pointed to the water pistols, now slowly leaking onto the lino. 'Not everyone can take a joke, mate.'

The air was relaxing. 'Oh sorry, Lionel. We were just mucking about. Funny, hey!' Sunny had remained silent throughout and I hadn't taken my eye off Ugly's gun — which was still aimed directly at Sunny. I nodded to Lionel. 'Maybe he could lower his gun as well?' I smiled.

Then Ugly started to smirk. 'You know, Lionel, I reckon these girls need to be taught a lesson.'

I was getting somewhat nervous now. So was Lionel. 'Nah. They're okay. Just a bit of fun. No harm done.' He did try. I always liked him for that.

'I reckon they need to be in the lock-up for a few hours. You know, let them think about what they've done here this afternoon.' He was almost licking his lips.

'Oh hey. We'll stop now. You win. We'll just go back to the pub and have a good lie-down. Okay?' I felt I had to say something. At least to give him the impression I wasn't intimidated by him. He still hadn't lowered his gun, though.

'Seems like they're resisting arrest to me, Lionel. Let's cuff them.' Lionel was completely thrown. Ugly had his cuffs out and had turned Sunny around before either Lionel or I could react. He pushed me in the shoulder and started to frogmarch Sunny down the corridor to the lock-up.

I followed with Lionel in step behind me. 'Hey. Don't do this. There's no need. We'll just go. Sorry. We didn't think you guys would take it quite so seriously.'

'Maybe you should check the roster before you try this again, Blondie.' Ugly was really enjoying this. He even slammed the lock-up gate shut with a loud clang. Just for further emphasis. Lionel apologised through the wire. But we knew he couldn't do anything. Ugly was senior to him. And vengeful.

So we sat. Side by side on the one bench, in the Halls Creek lock-up. It was a square of land with steel cyclone fencing around the perimeter and a three-walled corrugated-iron shed in one end of it. The shed was the only protection from the elements for the inmates and where they slept. The open yard meant that inmates could sit inside with their families on the outside. The lock-up was really only for short stays, overnight before bail or before further detention at Wyndham jail.

No one else was in. Only Sunny and me. The bench was hard, just a piece of wood. There were a few concrete slabs, big enough for one person to lie on, a tap for water — and that was all. For four hours. Four hours Ugly kept us in.

To begin with we sighed a bit. Then I walked round the square. Sunny hummed. Then sang Van Morrison. His whole *Best Of* album. I kept walking. Then she mentioned the noise — the one that had got their attention in the corridor. Then we argued. Then blamed each other for the idea in the first place. By this stage, one hour in, our heads were sore. Too much alcohol too early in the day.

Then we started wondering just how long he could keep us in there. This took the form of 'Fucking arsehole prick. It's been an hour already. Bastard.' And 'Surely not much longer. I mean really, who the fuck does he think he is? Fucking arsehole prick.' And reached 'I am not serving him again.' And 'Or his family. They come into the restaurant all the time.'

'Yeah but I feel sorry for his family. I mean, imagine what they have to live with.'

'Okay. I'll serve her and the kids but not him. Maybe we can get him barred from the pub.'

'What? You reckon fuckwit Call-Me-Alex would do that for us?'

Two hours and the sun was still hot out the back. Strange, because it was getting late. Must be something to do with the angle of the enclosure and the corrugated-iron roof. Reflections and a clear view straight to the western horizon dazzled and blinded our eyes. A beautiful sunset was preparing, except for the chequerboard patterning of the wire cage. We had settled into a resigned quiet.

Into the third hour, Sunny had Van Morrison on repeat and I was resisting the urge to tell her just what a right-wing conservative he was — in shorthand. That was when I remembered the Scotch. 'Hey, Sunny. You still have the hipflask?'

'Brilliant idea.'

So we passed Scotch between us for a while. Finished it too soon. I filled it up with water. We passed that back and forth. It was really quiet out here. We couldn't hear the town, or even the highway. It felt like we were in the middle of nowhere. Well, I guess we were, really. But even more removed. Separate. Isolated. That's when I got angry.

'Pip,' Sunny was saying as I sat swearing and kicking the concrete slab. 'Pip, it can't be for much longer. We aren't at his mercy. Someone else will come on. Don't worry. Just calm down and we'll be okay.'

But we *were* at his mercy. In much the same way that anyone locked up with or without good reason was at his mercy. Neither of them had come to check up on us. We could have been hanging from the beams out here and they wouldn't know. We had all our clothes. They hadn't taken our belts or socks or shirts. Easy.

My head was hurting and the setting sun was allowing a chill back into the air. It had been too long. I screamed.

'Pip. Shut up. Come on. It'll just make it worse.'

I screamed again. Well, it was more of a howl. Lionel came running out. Worried. Good.

Ugly followed him. 'Now, girls, you just hang in there. Lesson's not over yet.'

Lionel had already begun to unlock the gate. Ugly slammed the bolt back in. 'Come on, Constable. You've got filing to do.'

Sunny looked at me. She pulled me down next to her and put her arm round me. 'Maybe champagne breakfast wasn't such a good idea.' There was a swirl of cool desert air. And we both started to laugh. And then cry. And then laugh again. The sunset provided a distraction and we played hopscotch in the lengthening purple shadows. If you landed outside a shadow it meant buying a drink for the other person.

Finally, four hours, almost to the minute, later, Ugly unlocked the gate. 'You're free to go, girls. Thank you for your attendance. If you require further lessons on the proper etiquette of young ladies in police stations, don't hesitate to come again.' I was sure he couldn't even spell etiquette, let alone know what it meant. 'The first lesson was free.'

We walked out the gate, back into the station house, having to brush past him on the way. Lionel was at the desk. Trying not to look at us.

We walked out the door. The sun was nearly gone from the town. We headed up the street to the hotel. Neither of us said anything. Freedom. The cool air made me sigh. Sunny smiled. I smiled. Then we started running. Running down the middle of the road and screaming. We never did serve Ugly again.

WHITE JUSTICE

1990 saw the Royal Commission into Aboriginal Deaths in Custody still travelling across the nation to investigate the 99 Aboriginal and Torres Strait Islander deaths in police, prison or juvenile detention custody that had occurred between January 1980 and May 1989.

The Western Australian investigators swung through town while I was there. There had been one death in the Halls Creek lock-up and while the Aboriginal man had had an underlying health condition that police hadn't known about, there were still questions to answer about duty of care. As well as specific cases, the Commission was also looking at the underlying causes of deaths in custody, which included how alcohol was served to Aboriginal people. This put the hotel under scrutiny.

One evening, when I started my shift in the cocktail bar, three men, one of the bar managers and two cops, were sitting drinking. They'd already had two rounds of Scotch and it was just 5.30 pm. Must have been a long day, I thought.

About six o'clock the commissioner and a few of his team went into the restaurant for dinner. The three at my bar all looked across and clocked who it was, as they came through the door. The bar manager and one of the cops had given evidence to the Commission that day.

A table was set up for the commissioner and his staff and food orders were taken. All the while the three at my bar kept watching the group. Another round. Their fifth. A break in the restaurant muzak and there was only the sound of cutlery, glasses and muffled talking. And then one of the cops, leaning against the bar, started laughing. He slapped the cop next to him, 'Let's have a toast.'

'What for?' asked the manager.

'Because we can.'

The three of them almost choked with laughter. I stopped my cleaning and looked at them. They stood up, cheered loudly and skolled the rest of their drinks.

The commissioner couldn't help but hear. He looked across; some of his table kept their eyes on their plates, others just stared at each other in quiet disbelief, but the commissioner kept looking, staring back at the men intently with an unwavering gaze.

The three ordered another round.

ALICE TO KUNUNURRA

I was stuck in Alice Springs one late August weekend. I'd flown down with Tim, one of the fixed-wings, for a few days of casino sightseeing and the plane had broken down as we landed — no joke. Which meant that I had to catch a bus all the way back to Halls Creek to arrive in time for my shift on Monday.

It's a very weird bus trip. Up from Alice to Tennant Creek, then through Five Ways and Katherine, across to Timber Creek, Kununurra and then Halls Creek. It's a long journey, through desolate and sometimes disturbing country, with a curious mix of tourists and locals all herded together in close proximity.

The tourists, a group of six Americans ('When do we see the naked people, Bob?'), were taking photos of anything out the window and were generally tiresome. The locals, some white, some black, were mostly ignoring each other.

There was one young Aboriginal girl with her new baby who wasn't looking so good. The baby cried for much of the journey, except for when she dosed it with Baby Panadol. It was tiny. Too tiny for my peace of mind. The girl, who looked like a teenager, wasn't getting any rest or sleep and she was clearly exhausted.

At Katherine we stopped for a food break. By this stage I was well aware of the protocols around white people talking to Aboriginal people and vice versa. Especially in situations like this, where I didn't know the girl and she didn't know me. I, an unknown white woman, would not be spoken to or asked for help. But there was no older Aboriginal woman on the bus, just some older men and two young boys, none of whom would probably even speak to the woman. They would watch over her but would probably not actively help her.

So I decided to break all the protocols and see what happened. I bought two cups of hot tea and heaped sugar in one of them. The girl had stayed outside with her baby and was walking around trying to coax her to sleep. I walked up to her. 'Hi. I got you tea.' I held the cup out in front of me. The woman was unsure and instantly shy. I just kept steamrolling. 'It's hot and I hope you like sugar because I put quite a lot in.' I could tell there was a flicker of surprise but she hadn't backed off yet. 'Here, why don't I hold the baby while you sit down and drink your tea.' The older Aboriginal men had moved closer and were watching intently. 'Come on, I'll just walk up and down with her while you relax. Just till we have to get back on the bus.' She had been trying not to look at me, but now she looked me fully in the eyes.

I took a step closer and held out the tea. I carefully put my own tea down on the bench closest to us and said, 'Here you go. Sit right down here and tell me how to rock your baby.' I leaned into her so that if she offered me the baby there would be no time or space for hesitation. 'How old is she? She's so cute.' I turned my full attention to the baby and placed my hand gently on the swaddling. The woman didn't shy away. I was in.

Within a second I had the baby, the girl had the tea and she looked like she was about to cry — I just hoped it was in relief. So I nursed the baby while she sat and drank her tea and the old men watched us. Slowly, I figured out she was from Kununurra, she had been in Alice to be in hospital, the baby was two months old and had a cold. She had no family in Alice and even though she had received support from the hospital and some of the Alice Aboriginal women, she was exhausted. And she was only sixteen years old.

We got back on the bus and I asked her if it was all right if I sat next to her. She nodded. So I held the baby for pretty much the rest of the trip while she caught up on some sleep. We didn't talk much. The baby eventually slept a little and by the time we reached Kununurra they were both looking a bit better. Some women met her off the bus and she thanked me and waved goodbye.

A couple of months later an old Aboriginal woman came up to me in the pub. I was clearing some glasses and she handed me a card. I didn't know her or where she was from, but she said, 'For you, missus. From Sandy. From Kununurra. With baby. You remember?'

I didn't for a minute but then of course it all came back. 'Oh, that's really nice of her. How's she doing?'

We sat down and the old lady told me how they were getting on. Apparently all was going well. Sandy and the baby were well and the father was hanging around and had a job.

The old lady told me about Sandy's family and her relations in Halls Creek. I asked how Sandy knew it was me — we hadn't swapped names. The grandmother cracked a smile. 'Everyone know you, Blondie. Easy.'

I had to smile. But the amount of effort it had taken for Sandy to send the card, or to ask someone to send the card or even for the Aboriginal woman to decide to give it to me, was quite extraordinary. And humbling. We hugged.

SUNG

Alvin's wife had just had their third child. She was in the hospital and he was in the bar. Pissed. I had seen him before in the street. He was an easy smiler. Always grinning. And his eyes sparkled. He and his mates, cousin-brothers, in the bar were fun. Joking. Spinning yarns. Laughing. Acting up. And trying to get a rise out of me. It was pretty funny actually.

A couple of days later I was coming back from Jean-Paul's and I saw Alvin and his friends on the street. I had my camera with me and had been taking yet more photos of the stark blue arch of endless sky and the dusty green of eucalypts. Alvin called out to me.

'Hey, Blondie. Take our photo.' I stopped and turned towards them. 'Come on, Blondie. Take our photo.' He was grinning and his friends were shyly giggling. 'Take our photo so you remember us.'

How could I refuse? 'Okay. Over there in front of the tree.'

They reacted like schoolchildren, all tumbling over to the

tree. Joking, pushing and tripping each other. 'Okay, bunch up together. And smile.' The three of them all pulled faces. I laughed, took the photo. 'There you go. All done.'

'Take another one, miss. Take another one.'

I laughed despite myself. 'Okay. Line up, pretend to be serious.' Three photos later I said enough.

'Thank you, missus,' Alvin said as he grabbed my hand. His skin felt cool and dry, like paper.

'Hey, Blondie. I'm going to sing you. Your name Pip. Yeah.'

I shook my head, turned and walked away. 'See you guys later.'

The next night I couldn't sleep. It was a warm night, warmer than we'd had before. Sleep wouldn't come. As soon as I closed my eyes and started to doze it felt as though there was something pressing, urgent in the back of my mind. Some idea I couldn't or didn't want to dream.

The following day I was cranky. That sleep-deprived, scratchy, tired mood. I was removed from the everyday. Just going through the motions.

That evening Alvin came into the front bar. By himself. Lea was working with me, and Elvis was sitting drinking at the saloon bar, keeping us company. Alvin reached through the opening in the mesh and called out my name. 'Hey, Pip. Hey, Pip. I sing you. You my wife now. You give me drink.'

I looked at Lea. 'Nah, Alvin. I am so not your wife. You've already got one of those. And if you haven't got any money you aren't getting a drink.'

Lea wasn't prone to overreacting, and she didn't. She glanced at Alvin and kept working. Elvis, on the other hand, could get excited easily. He stood up on his chair to look around into the front bar and see who was calling out to me. 'Hey, Alvin. You really sing Pip?'

'She right, mate. She mine now.'

Elvis glanced at me.

'Elvis. I don't believe that shit for a minute. He's just stirring me up.'

Elvis held my gaze. 'And how do you feel, Pip?'

Lea stopped and reached for Elvis's hand. 'Don't spin her shit, Elvis.'

'Could be worse, Pip. At least he lives in town. Otherwise you'd be stuck out in the desert.'

I loved Elvis but I still hadn't quite figured out when he was taking the piss. 'I don't believe in singing. Just don't. If there's anything to it, it's psychosomatic. And really. Alvin has no hold over me.'

Elvis was still looking at me intently. 'Right.'

'Hey, Pip,' Alvin called. 'Hey, Pip, my missus she pretty mad that I've got me another wife. She might come down here for a fight.'

'Alvin. Go away. You haven't sung me. I'm not your wife. Leave the bar now.' I was angry. Especially if he had told his wife and she was going to turn up wanting to sort me out. 'Your wife is in hospital with your new baby. Go and visit her.'

Alvin smiled. 'Your eyes so blue. That's what got me. Miss Blue Eyes.' As he left the bar he laughed; it rang like a musical note, lasting and gaining strength. I could still hear it ten minutes later.

When we were cleaning up that night I asked Lea what she thought. 'I don't know, Pip. But what I do know is that the people up here know lots of things we don't. They see lots of things we don't and they can make you do lots of things you wouldn't otherwise do. But you'll know. You'll feel it if he has sung you. Or whatever he has done. I mean he's already planted this seed in your mind. Hasn't he? Simple.'

I couldn't sleep again that night.

I saw Elvis over breakfast. 'I'm feeling weird about this singing business,' I said.

Elvis nodded. 'Yeah. I mean you should. That's the point really.'

'But I'm not going to marry him. I'm not going to stay here. This isn't my life.' The sighing of the just-boiled kettle was the only sound.

'Well,' said Elvis, 'I guess it isn't. But it could be. I mean, it really could be. Seriously.'

We sat in silence and finished our sausages and eggs.

'So what do I do about it? How do I stop him?'

'We need to find someone to unsing you.'

At lunch Elvis came back and said that Tom could do it. Tom was an old man in town. Respected. He knew Alvin and was related to him in some way. Tom came to see me. He held my hand, told me I had beautiful eyes and left. 'Is that it, Elvis?'

Elvis shrugged. 'Don't worry. You don't need to do anything. He'll put things back the way they were. Just trust him.'

It was odd. While I didn't have faith or believe in the singing, I had to believe in the 'unsinging' to be sure it worked.

I slept deeply and long that night. And while Alvin came in a few times afterwards, there was something different. Different in how he looked and how we related to each other. He never called me 'wife' again. And I did feel different.

Somehow more present in the world than I had for those few days. It is a difficult thing to explain. That feeling of being removed without being physically absent.

I can still remember the way I felt when I woke up that morning. Like a fresh, new person.

NIGHT BASKETBALL

Three professional basketball players from the Perth Wildcats were in town. They had come up to do some workshops at the school, and they were staying at the hotel for a week. Two of the guys were white Australians and the third was an African-American who had played professionally in the United States and was over playing in Australia for a year.

The American player, John, was interested in the local Aboriginal community and wanted to meet some of the kids. Of course, the workshops were a great hit and the level of school attendance shot up that week. He was followed wherever he went by adoring young children.

One evening John asked if I would take him on a tour of the town. He'd heard that the kids played basketball on the council courts at night and wanted to see if they were playing tonight.

We headed towards the basketball court, which at night glowed with fluorescent lights. There were about twenty kids, all boys, black, playing a game while others watched. As we drew closer one of the boys saw John coming. We were besieged. Yells and cries of excitement, quickly followed by embarrassment, shyness. They all backed off. John was a hero to them, a god. Someone from another planet.

He got them throwing baskets and gave them some tips and then they started playing a game. A few of the boys watching stood near me. One of them, cheeky as and all of twelve, leaned over and whispered, 'So you with him now, miss? You his missus?'

I smiled. 'No. John's a friend. Just a friend. He wanted someone to bring him down here to meet you guys. That's all.'

The boy smiled and whispered something to his two friends. About an hour later John and I headed back to the hotel.

It was clear the next morning that word had whipped around about my night tour. Call-Me-Alex cornered me when I was with Elvis. 'So, how was your walk?'

'Fine, Alex. And quite safe.'

'Yeah, but you know the rules. No walking around at night.'

'Yes. But a guest, and a well-known guest with a public profile, asked me to take him to meet the boys on the courts. That's what we did. And really, if I'm not safe walking around with a big black man in this town, then there's no hope.' I shot a look at Elvis who was trying not to laugh.

Call-Me-Alex had his half-lech, half-smile face on. 'Well you'd know about that one, Blondie. But consider this yet another warning.'

Of course, I didn't pay any attention to him at all. Especially as I was the golden girl with all the kids in town — and some of the mothers. They all wanted to know about John, and I was riding high in their eyes. I was suddenly very cool.

SIGNS OF LIFE

One morning I was walking up the road from the hotel to the shops when I noticed an Aboriginal woman being trailed by an Aboriginal man. She seemed to be stopping intermittently and he was clearly awkward and anxious but not able to touch her or speak to her. I inadvertently caught up with them, because they were moving slower than I was, and the man, although shy, looked at me questioningly. I didn't know what was going on and certainly didn't want to get involved in some domestic, so I just kept walking without speaking to him.

The woman was a couple of paces ahead of me when she stopped again and bent over; it was an odd movement because she seemed to be arching her back at the same time as doubling over. She was clearly in pain. I decided I had to ask. 'Hey, missus. You okay?' She looked at me, embarrassed even in her pain, but then the pain seemed to disappear from her body. I realised she was in the later stages of childbirth.

'Hey, missus. The hospital's up here, not far now. You can

make it.' She smiled at me, just as another wave of pain hit her. She crouched lower and planted her feet firmly onto the ground. Oh my God, I thought,she's going to have the baby here. On the side of the road. FUCK. What do I do?

I was working up a panic when she looked at me again and said, 'She fine, missus.'

I leaned down next to her. 'I'll run to the hospital and get help.' She grabbed my arm as another wave of pain hit her. And she wasn't letting go. I looked at the man but he was three paces away and clearly not getting any closer. And then, within what seemed like both the longest three minutes and the quickest three minutes of my life, I was holding a newborn baby. A tiny, tiny squealing girl.

I held her out for the mother to hold and she smiled, hugging the baby to her chest. Then she just stood up and kept walking. I was stunned. I hurried after her and stayed beside her the remaining 800 metres or so to the hospital. I told the nurses what had happened and that the afterbirth would be out any minute with this woman's constitution. The head nurse knew the woman, Elsie, and said they had been expecting her on the Flying Doctor two days ago. Elsie laughed and said, 'Missed that fellow.' The nurses led her off to deliver the afterbirth and she waved at me as she hugged her baby.

I turned and walked out of the hospital, stunned. The man, her husband I assumed, was standing at the bottom of the stairs. Not wanting to get any closer to the whitefella sick house.

I smiled at him. 'She's good, mate. They're fine. They're both fine.' I shook his hand. 'She's amazing.'

We both sat down on the top step, me totally overcome with relief and surprise and the new father beaming.

PAYBACKS ARE BITCHES

For a long time there had been a feud in Halls Creek between two Aboriginal families, with regular, though infrequent, altercations. The feud calmed down when a son of one of the families was convicted and jailed for assaulting a *gadiya* woman at Halls Creek. He was one of the reasons why no one from the pub was meant to walk around the town at night — well, no *gadiya* woman anyway.

With him being locked up for a few years, his family had lost a sizeable chunk of face. But the word was he was getting out of Wyndham jail and was likely to head home to Halls Creek. And apparently he was angry. Wanted vengeance. So the police all over the district were getting edgy. Everyone was trying to second-guess him. And the families.

To add to this, it was the end of the football season, the grand final was approaching and it would be easy for one person to go unnoticed in the gathering crowds of fans.

The weekend he was getting out, the teams were all playing in Kununurra, and Halls Creek was empty. It was quite a relief really. Over the previous few days everyone had gradually headed off. Locals, out-of-towners, whites, blacks, even the police, who had either taken time off or had been rostered on for a shift in Kununurra. The police thought that if the 'Unknown Quantity', to use their phrase, did turn up, it would be at Kununurra to catch up with his relatives and to 'probably' start a fight.

So by Saturday the Halls Creek streets were empty and the bars quiet. I had been left with the promise of a faxed identity picture and some backup — of what sort I wasn't sure — but I wasn't really worried. I figured that the situation was nothing more than a family grievance which could be easily provoked by cops.

So there I was, opening up the bar; happy, knowing I had hours and hours of quiet. No music. No irritated, aggravated, demanding customers. Just me. Time to think.

I cleaned the bar. I stood out the front of the hotel listening to the crows across the road. I stopped and watched the dust curl in the hot day with the cool breeze which would build into a wind come afternoon. I thought about the fact that the desert looked the same no matter what the season — except for the winter beanies and coats.

I had a couple of customers. Three actually. Two at opening who didn't stay around. Recovering from the night before and realising that they were missing the main action in Kununurra. The other one, a guy, came in about one in the afternoon. He had a good look around. I said, 'Hey, mate, everyone's in Kununurra. Football.' He nodded and walked out the side entrance. And came back. He had a nice smile. Asked for an Emu.

'You from round here?' I asked. 'Yeah, but not for a while. What's changed?'

And then we started chatting. I said I'd only been here a few months and that even in that time I had noticed a change in how the town was going.

'Yeah? And what's that?' he said.

'Oh, I don't know. Maybe I'm exaggerating but I think the tension's rising.'

'Yeah?' he commented. And looking me full in the face: 'You think so?'

I laughed self-consciously. Suddenly realising how ridiculous it must seem to a black man to hear that from a *gadiya* woman.

So the subject was changed. I passed him the latest newspapers. I sold him drinks. We discussed life. The desert, grandmothers, lovers and children. Had a great time. And I remained on the selling-of-alcohol side and he remained on the drinking-of-alcohol side. He never seemed drunk. He never asked questions about my life, about me. I didn't ask any direct questions about his life. He had a child, he'd been away for a few years (down south, I thought) and was looking forward to sharing their life again.

About six o'clock or so, he said he had to go, to get a lift. We shook hands. And I mean we shook hands, as in the secret insider handshake. Lots of fists and bonding. I'd been taught it by The Joker, the pool player. Of course Billy — he said his name was Billy — was impressed. 'Hey, Billy, nice to chat. See you round.'

Throughout the day I had had a series of phone calls from Darren, the duty bar manager, about the fax that the police were sending through from Kununurra and it wasn't working. 'Maybe get them to send the 'BEWARE' fax from Wyndham,' I suggested. 'If it is just photos it's going to be pretty unclear anyways — I mean, he is black after all.'

'Blondie,' said Darren, 'we don't think you're taking this threat seriously.'

'But,' I insisted, 'there is no threat until someone makes one.' Exasperated, he gave up trying to argue with me.

It wasn't until later — maybe nine o'clock — that a few of the locals turned up and Darren came down from the office for a drink with them. He brought a fax with him. 'Hey, Blondie, this is Madman's photo. If he turns up we just need to let the police know. We can't do anything about it but they want to know where he is.'

He handed me the fax. I looked at it carefully as I poured him his usual — rum and Coke, no ice.

'Right. And when did he get out of Wyndham?' I asked.

'Just yesterday morning. The cops reckon he's in Kununurra stirring trouble.'

'Right,' I said. 'And what did he do exactly?'

'Well,' said Darren looking straight at me, 'he assaulted a woman. A white woman. And almost killed her.'

'Hmmm.' I was transfixed by the fax. While the photo was a bad photo, profile and close and ugly, I still wanted to know more. 'And what do they think he'll do? I mean, it's family, isn't it? It's personal, right?'

The five people in the bar, two couples and Darren, were all looking at me. 'Pip, what does it matter what he might do? He had already caused lots of shit long before he went to jail. Just watch out for him.' Darren was just starting with his 'stupid female' tone.

'Okay,' I said. 'Does watching out for him mean I tell you that he spent all afternoon — from about one until, God I don't know, a couple of hours before you lot arrived — in this bar talking to me?'

The silence grew and mustered force. 'So who was watching out for me?' I said. Possibly a little too loud.

The on-duty, bare-minimum police came really fast. To tell the truth I thought it was a bit of overkill, but it was definitely the fastest they had ever answered a call to the pub. Obviously *gadiya* women under potential threat got them going.

I was ferried to the police station, had a 'post' outside my bedroom door at night, phone calls all patched through the main commander system, not allowed outside the hotel grounds until they caught him.

And they did catch him. Seven days after he got out of jail. He was arrested for assault of another *gadiya* woman. A girl who worked in a pub. Not in Halls Creek, but all the same. Close.

Especially when Elvis told me that the victim had also had a relationship with Eric, the Aboriginal guy I'd been 'involved' with. Eric was related to the rival family. Was the woman payback? Or perhaps simply showing he was capable of anything, of reinforcing that threat, that was payback. Or perhaps the feeling that remains with me is payback. The feeling of dark menace, of turmoil and the charm of the unknown, of danger.

DESERT DRIVING

Simon was always hassling me about going to Wyndham to see him, rather than relying on his visits to Halls Creek for us to catch up. So eventually I made the drive through the desert, about four hours of well-maintained highway with one turn to the left as the road splits to run north-east to Kununurra or north-west to Wyndham.

He had a studio, a corrugated-iron shed really, down near the water, almost on the edge of the Timor Sea. We sat and looked at his hessian-covered shed walls, with his landscapes and portraits scattered across them, as the breeze lifted the dust and swirled patterns in the front door, and we laughed about the big old saltwater crocodile that stole tourists' dogs from the pier, despite the warning signs telling people not to take their dogs down there.

One day Simon announced he was going to have a party, and Jim, Sarah, Sunny and I all decided to go.

We took two vehicles, Jim driving his Toyota ute and Sunny

and I in a smaller borrowed ute. Distance isn't the same out there. Of course we would drive a round trip of eight hours for a party. It never crossed our minds not to.

We left Halls Creek late in the afternoon. Arrived along with fifty or so others from across the Kimberley. Drank. Smoked. Partied. And then, about four in the morning, I left. Snuck out. Drove back to Halls Creek.

Still pissed. Driving down the middle of the road so I didn't run into any cattle or hit any people walking on the side. Driving slowly. Meandering. Watching the stars fade and dawn rise. Listening to the birds. Feeling the freedom of driving on a straight road, with only the horizon to aim for. That feeling of being insignificant but involved. Another story in the grand epic of the desert. But still a story. And watching the desert unfold before me. For me. Loving the air. And the driving. The bitumen and the tyres and the wind.

At the turn-off to Halls Creek I came across two white contractors' vans. The four men were sitting out the back of the vans, watching television. They had a great big satellite dish trained at the heavens and they were glued to the set. I slowed down and threw my arm out the window in a long, slow wave. The men turned their heads and looked, one raised his hand as though from habit, not acknowledgement, as I floated by and the sound of a foreign language, French perhaps, echoed through the dawn.

I have always been grateful for that experience. Those hours of just me and the space above the desert floor. Of the colours and the distance. The absence of activity. Wrapped in the surety of horizon. In the knowledge of sunrise. Of course Simon roasted me when he realised I had left. Drunk. And driving.

BRAWL

After the football season came the rodeo and racing season. The showground was out on the eastern edge of town, a large circle of dust marked out with the white fence posts of the ring and the faded bleachers of the grandstand.

Halls Creek rodeo meant lots of people. Lots of cowboys. Lots of talk and money. Lots of loving and lots of fighting.

And of course there were damaged horses and damaged bulls, shot in the back pens. Bloody, gouged and broken boys. Dust. Fried food. Cheap beer. And as night descended the fights would start. Families against families. Lovers against lovers. Strangers against strangers. Brothers on brothers.

The rodeo started Friday and went to Sunday night. The pub ran the bars and food stall which meant I was out there working. Jim and Sarah, as part of the organising committee, were helping out. Late Saturday we were about to head back into town after a long day. Sarah and I were locking up the bar under the grandstand and Jim was checking all the other doors and entrances. We were the only people left, apart from a couple of cowboys watering their horses.

As Sarah and I walked out to Jim's ute, the last vehicle in the parking lot, we saw an Aboriginal man running in our direction towards the buildings. And a distance behind him, in a ball of red dust, was a gang of thirty or so men. All pursuing him. As he passed us we could hear his breathing, hard and fast. It sounded as though he had been running for a while.

Jim stepped around the corner of the concrete bar as the man reached him. The guy just kept running past him. Didn't even look at him. Sarah screamed at Jim. Jim looked at us and saw the gang of men almost level with us. I could smell the fear and the bodies. The sweat and the excitement. Jim started to gesture at us, yelling. As we reached the ute, Sarah unlocked the door quickly, and the men passed us in a cloud of dust, with a low murmur of energy and threat.

We got in the ute and locked the doors. It was suddenly eerie. Quiet. The late shadows dropping a purple blanket on the grounds. The dust settling. 'If they catch him he's going to be dead,' Sarah said. Shit. She gunned the engine and drove as close to the back of the buildings as possible. 'Stay here. Keep the engine running.' She was out the door before I could stop her. Shit.

I crawled into the driver's seat and watched. I could just see through the cattle gates to the grandstand and the bar. Jim had climbed the gate and was sitting high up on the top of the fence, trying to calm the crowd down. Without success. They were ignoring him and had spread out and started banging on doors and walls. Kicking open shutters and denting roller doors. Making disturbing, out-of-control noises. Banging.

Smashing. I couldn't see Sarah. But I could hear police sirens. Coming our way. Bloody hell. As if that was going to help.

I saw a movement in the corner of the rear-view mirror. Behind me. It was the man. The pursued man. He had been hiding under the bank of seating and was working his way up to climbing into the back of the ute. Shit. But then, I thought, what option did he have? They would find him and they would hurt him. There weren't that many places to hide.

Three police vans sped in through the gates of the grounds. There was no way out now — for any of us. The cops drove up to the buildings and slid to a stop, half blocking off the road. They jumped out with their guns in their hands. Oh sweet Jesus.

The engine was still going. I revved it just in case and I felt the man get in the back. I didn't look as he pulled the tarpaulin over his body and crawled deep into the darkness and limited safety of the covered tray. I didn't really want to know.

Sarah suddenly appeared at the window, I unlocked the door and she climbed in. Locking it after her. We both sat there breathing heavily. Watching.

The six police (they had to be joking — they were outnumbered five to one) had walked into the buildings and were yelling for the guys to stop and come out of wherever they were hiding. The police knew who they were and were calling out their names. Brothers, apparently. Chasing another brother.

I saw Jim, still on the fence. I wound the window down and reversed so I could turn and edge closer to him. 'Jim. Get in here, man,' I yelled at him.

He glanced across, saw me coming and began to climb down. Sarah unlocked the door and moved over to the centre. It felt as though we had one chance and that was all. And it worked. Jim hit the ground running, dived for the open door and we sped off. Dust behind and no damage done. The cops let us through, waved us on, and went back to biding their time till the gang got bored, gave up and went back to the pub.

The three of us were all in shock. 'They were really going to do him over,' said Sarah.

Jim just shook his head. 'Not a chance. He won't stand a chance.'

I was breathing harder, nervous now. Because inadvertently we had intervened. Something I had always been told not to do.

'I think he'll be okay. At least for now.' My hands were sweating on the wheel. Those guys had meant business.

'Nah. The cops will just wait and watch. They aren't going to stop it,' said Jim.

'Maybe not. But as he is now in the back of the ute, they won't find him.'

Jim whipped around to see if it was true. Of course the guy was still in hiding. 'Shit, Pip.'

'Hey, it wasn't me — he just jumped in. Right before you got off the fence. I wasn't getting out to tell everyone where he was.' Shit.

We pulled up in a dark street near the hospital. With scrub around but close to the highway. Near the roadhouses so he could get a lift. If he wanted. Dark enough so no one would know he had been rescued by us. We got out. Jim uncovered the back. A young guy, so scared he could have passed for white, sprang onto the ground. He took one look at us and ran towards the highway.

ANOTHER WORLD

The tap, tap, tap of a coin on stainless steel. Hey, miss, two boat wine. The thin film of dust smudges in a curve of the steel as some of the sticky liquid spills into the plastic cups. Two cups. Through the gap in the mesh, the cage, keeping us safe, keeping us in, keeping us separate. Dark dry hands, burnished red, reach for the drinks. Thanks, miss.

Everything has the red layer, the dust. Surfaces, people, inside washing machines, glass washers, linen cupboards. We must be breathing so much of it. Must be in our lungs, living in our veins and capillaries. At the back of our eyes. The metho swishes as the coins go in. My hands feel clean and rubbery soft as I pull them out and turn to the next customer. Green can, missus. Two green cans, miss.

It is a slow hot afternoon in the saloon bar. I wonder about myself. This town. These people. I wonder about my feeling of confinement. Containment. I can see the grid of the town's streets in my mind. Branded into my dreams. Weird feeling hemmed in with all this space, the desert, around me. But the country is unknowable, indefinable, just out of reach. For me at any rate. I realise I stay in the well-worn boundaries of the white known.

Later, in the pool bar, as I sit with Jean-Paul, watching *gadiya* customers swim and sun themselves in a separate world to the one in the front bars, I ask him what we are here for. '*Mon Dieu*, daahlink — the lifestyle, of course!' He smiles. 'Skyzz blue for dayzz,' his French accent rolling his words and cigarette in his mouth.

I remember what Roger, the bus driver, said all those months ago. I start to think seriously about leaving, sitting there in the shadows of palm trees as the setting sun casts orange across the sky. And I realise I have already left.

THREE-CROWNED JACK

He was a slip of a boy. With a body not quite caught up to his age. Sandy hair, freckles and bare feet. We met at the rodeo. He had to go down to Meekatharra for some work and then he was going to come back through to Darwin. I asked if I could get a ride. 'Sure,' Jack said. 'I'll be back in a week.'

The wet was threatening. The slow build-up of humidity could be felt even this far into the dry dust of the Kimberley, and tempers were flaring. It was time to go. To get out before the big wet. Before it started to rain and the floods left no escape.

I had left the pub a week before — resigned before they could sack me. Darren, the blond manager I had disliked from the moment he had picked me up at the roadhouse all those months before, wouldn't let a group of Aboriginal women into the cocktail bar because they weren't dressed according to regulations. I had had enough. We argued. I left.

I walked to the roadhouse and got a job. But after one shift

I knew it wasn't for me. And I had thought the pub was bad. Grease and heat and harassment from the management. Being told matter-of-factly to serve *gadiyas* ahead of blackfellas. People gossiping about me, both black and *gadiya*, in front of me. It was definitely time to go.

When Jack came back through Halls Creek, that was it. I left. Sunny came as well, which was a relief. It meant it wasn't just me. I wasn't the only one going mad.

It felt like we were escaping. Sneaking out. We left quietly, saying our goodbyes in one night with promises of letters and phone calls. Sarah and Jim announced they were going to get married in Darwin in November — none of us was going to miss that party — but 'See you in a couple of months' was really all that any of us could say. Sarah was really upset. Jim unable to show it and Sunny and I in Jack's ute, waving madly before we realised we were actually leaving.

But as soon as we were out of the town, beyond the green highway signs and maintained kerbs, it felt right to leave. To have come. And to know we would probably never return.

Jack was beautiful. Really. He had a quiet confidence and an intelligence beyond his years. A gentleness. And he just wanted to drive. He had come from somewhere and had somewhere to go. But the drive was the point.

Three-Crowned Jack had been given his name because he had been able, since before he could remember, to walk on cat's-eyes. Barefoot. Cat's-eyes — hard, thick, knife-sharp prickles. Barefoot. Without any damage to his feet. Even as a toddler. Now his soles were as thick and soft as leather. Most everyone had heard of him. Liked him. And as a consequence Sunny and I were treated like royalty along the road.

And we drove. Through Kununurra. Through the boab forest. Past anthills, red dirt and haunting humanlike shadows, as Jack told us the Dreaming story about the upturned pregnant woman, destined always to swell with her head in the ground. Alongside Victoria River with its dull grey water and mauve sunrise. Jack quietly showing us what to look for. What to see. And we slept. Safe in a bubble of warm air created by this gentle creature.

We stopped at Timber Creek. Just inside the Northern Territory border and it felt different. The land. The people. The weather. The heat. There was more dampness, more moisture in their humour and their bitterness. Another rodeo weekend. Sunny and I scored shifts at the Timber Creek Hotel. Alternate ones, I was on days, Sunny on nights, and Jack kicked around with his older brothers. Monday morning the three of us got back into the ute. Tired. Hungover. Sore. Wanting to put distance between them and us.

Outside of Katherine, we stopped to have a cup of tea with Jack's mother, an Aboriginal woman. Neither Sunny nor I had had any idea. Jack was fair. His brothers were all fair. She was so pleased to see us. To see Jack. He was happy to make her happy. As we were driving out her driveway Jack began to tell us the story of his mother and his father. How his father, a *gadiya* man, owned some of the land we were driving through. How his father had had less and less to do with his mother.

Jack described how his two brothers had left their mother, physically and emotionally, as they grew up. Now they were bachelors in demand. Money and land. 'And arseholes, judging by their behaviour on the weekend,' said Sunny. She'd been at the receiving end of one of his brother's attention nonstop for the 48 hours we were in town. Jack grinned. He also loved his brothers.

Katherine and then Darwin. Dinner with Jack and then a goodbye. To him. To the desert. To the road.

MATARANKA

HOT AND HUMID

I'd never heard of Mataranka but it was the only place the Darwin agency had two jobs going. So Sunny and I took them.

Mataranka is a small town, an hour south of Katherine on the Stuart Highway, and in 1990 it had only about 150 permanent residents. It had two pubs (a locals' pub, the Old Elsey Inn, and one for the tourists, the Homestead), a roadhouse, a café, a police station, a motel with beautiful peacocks, and a couple of streets of houses scattered west of the highway. Its main claim to fame was the natural thermal springs at the Mataranka Homestead, where a tourist hotel had been built. And that it was the capital of the Never Never — the country where Jeannie Gunn lived and wrote her stories about life out on a station in 1902. Stories I loved as a child.

Mataranka had also, for many years, served as a stopping-off point for sick, old, infirm or pregnant Aboriginal people going in and out of south-east Arnhem Land. It was the nearest southern town to that region. In fact, nearly everyone, cattlemen, police, the station owners, tourists, shire staff, black and white, lived out on the land somewhere. Out of town. Out of sight of the scrubby trees and the ribbon of highway that linked the north to the south.

So when Sunny and I arrived to work at the Old Elsey Inn, the feel of the town was remarkably different to Halls Creek. It was transient. People moving. Tourists passing through. It felt as though the main action was happening elsewhere. That there was no centre. No reason for the town to exist.

We arrived on the bus. On a Monday afternoon. Dropped on the highway, directly opposite the entrance to the pub. After looking right, left, then right again to make sure that in fact there really was nothing else moving on the road, except for the disappearing bus heading to Alice Springs, we crossed the road with all our bags and struggled into the dimly lit bar.

'Hi. Are Peter or Paula about?'

The two punters sitting either end of the bar turned to look at us. The older, less unkempt one of them nodded towards the bar. 'In the office.'

I looked at Sunny, she shrugged. 'Thanks,' I said, and ducked under the bar and turned right into the thin doorway of a cupboard which constituted the office.

A big white-haired man was sitting at a desk. He turned to look at me. 'Peter? I'm Pip — one of the new bar staff. Sunny's outside.'

He stood up. 'Gidday.' He had a blustery, red drinker's complexion. He shook my hand. Seemed straightforward. No rules so far.

He showed the two of us to a row of old weathered demountable rooms at the side of the pub. 'These are your rooms, girls. Hope they'll be okay.' It must have been quite clear from our reaction that they wouldn't be. The windows didn't quite shut. And we could see the sad old springs of the beds from the doorway. We baulked. Obviously it wasn't the first time Peter had had this reaction but he seemed unsure about what to do next.

Just then a big white old Statesman pulled up and parked near the rooms. 'Hey, girls. I'm Paula. How are you going? Now, don't you worry about these rooms,' her brown mane of hair bouncing, her tight T-shirt distracting and her short shorts leaving not much to the imagination. Not bad for a 50-year-old. She went on, 'It's only for a couple of nights till the big house comes up again.' She pointed to a house a short distance away from the pub. 'You'll be fine up there. It's a lovely house. Now, it's nearly four o'clock, which one of you is going to start with nights?'

That would be me. Sunny needed to sleep. She was better on days than me anyway. Not many people asked for food at night. Sunny could whip up a steak sandwich in no time. Me, it was a real trial with no guarantees of an end result. And the smell of the roadhouse still haunted me. I didn't even have time for a shower before Paula wanted me in the bar.

FIRST NIGHTS

The two old punters already in the bar were Sam and Kurt. And they didn't like each other. Clearly. Kurt, the older, weather-beaten one who had been most helpful when we first arrived, worked around the pub. Maintenance and ordering supplies. Sam, a small weedy man with peppery scrub for a beard and a pink tongue that regularly licked his lips, lived at the pub and occasionally hosed down the concrete pavement of the garden area. Nice to meet you, I thought. Neither one the talkative type.

The dim wood-panelled room was cut in half by a stepped bar, beer and spirits on one side, punters on the other. The far right-hand side of the bar had a small hatch which was where the Aboriginal people were served. The ones from the transit camp, the ones just passing through. There were some who came into the bar itself but not many, unless they were in town with their white bosses.

The Inn had a cavernous kitchen with a huge old gas stove in it where the meals were cooked — basic fare: steak sandwiches, egg-and-bacon rolls, burgers. I felt nervous in the kitchen. Something about the size of it. And the very old, very large blue-tongue lizard, Stumpy, who would quietly appear while I was cooking. Stumpy made me feel I was being watched and added to the pressure to perform.

It felt slightly uncomfortable, this bar. Smaller than Halls Creek. A box with a low roof and small doorway. It felt tired. Almost sour. Or maybe that was just me.

Gradually the bar filled. 'So you're the new girl, hey. Blondie, isn't it?' asked a truckie, stopping for a quick beer or three on his way to Alice.

'Right. News travels fast then,' I said.

'Yeah,' said the truckie, who had a barrel for a chest and a mop for a hairdo. 'Especially when the news is about the new girls serving at the Old Elsey.'

His tone was overly familiar. It felt as though he knew me. Knew more about me than I wanted him to. The room became almost claustrophobic.

'You make it seem like a sentence,' I smart-mouthed back.

The truckie just winked at me. 'Keep it up, girlie. You'll be fine.'

The pub was busy for a Monday night. The garden area filled up with men and women, husbands and wives, girlfriends, all eating out. Calling the open-air slab of concrete with a couple of bougainvillea pots around it 'the garden area' is perhaps embellishing, but you get the idea. And it did have coloured light bulbs strung across the ceiling. Quite festive on a busy night.

The bar was the domain of the men. The phone, on the side of the bar, kept ringing and I kept answering it. I took to yelling out names and waiting for responses. 'Davo! Your wife is on the phone. Davo!' or 'It's for Trevor. Which Trevor? I don't know — you ask her.' And it was usually a female voice on the other end of the phone. Looking for a boyfriend or husband. I learned most of the local blokes' names that night. And heard way too much about their private lives.

Sunny came in about nine o'clock, warily looking about. 'How's it going?' she whispered, nodding in the direction of the drinkers.

I smiled and sighed. 'It's a small bar in the middle of nowhere. Same old, same old.'

She cracked a half-hearted grin. 'God, look at us.'

The entire bar had noticed Sunny. As was always the way. The truckie yelled across the tops of the heads of the drinkers, 'And this must be The Kid.'

Sunny turned to look at him.

'Yeah, Sunny. They've heard about us,' I explained. She didn't stay long.

The pub closed at midnight. I started to clean and close up about eleven when the crowd had dispersed. 'So how was your first night then?' a voice called from a table of men as I cleaned the garden area. I turned, arms full of glasses and dirty ashtrays. They were all looking at me. The four of them couldn't have been older than 30, and two were possibly only the same age as me.

'Fine. Everyone behaved themselves. How was yours?' I moved away to the next table.

'Well, I reckon ours was fine, fellas, don't you think? Especially with the new hired help to look at.'

Here we go, I thought. There always had to be one. 'Yeah,' I shot back, 'I guess it's better than staying home and looking at your wife.'

Damn it, Pip. Just shut up for once. I glanced at the table. The four of them were trying not to laugh.

'Not bad, Blondie. Not bad.' The same voice and the same smug tone. At least they could take a joke — even if I couldn't. As I headed back inside with my tray of glasses, I tried to remember his name from the phone call he had received earlier; it had been a woman, a young voice with a broad country accent.

The bar had emptied and I closed and locked the front doors from the inside. One night down. Turning back to the bar I realised that the guy from outside, the one who had spoken to me, was standing watching me. 'Last drinks, okay?'

'Sure. The same?'

'Yep, plus a fifth.'

'What's the fifth one drinking?'

'Not sure. I reckon a gin and tonic should do it though.'

I looked at him, big frame, square jaw, broad face, sun-lined, handsome. Something broken or resigned about him. 'I'll bring them right out.' He smiled and his face cracked in half. A grin so wide it revealed a gold tooth, front and centre.

'Righto.' He disappeared back out to the table.

I put the tray of four rums and the gin and tonic down on their table. 'Last drinks, boys.'

As I turned to go back inside, the same guy spoke again. 'Aren't you drinking yours?'

I couldn't help it, I had to smile. He was trying really hard. 'That's for me?'

'Gin and tonic all right?'

'Should do the trick.' One of the others, one of the younger ones, got up and grabbed a chair for me. Nice. 'So, since you know my name — who are you lot?' They all laughed. The ice was broken as the desert chill snuck over me. It was cold. Still. The warm days are misleading, I thought, and shivered.

The Charmer, that's what I christened him, introduced them all. Rob, dark, slim and ready for a fight; Tom, the tall, easygoing redhead; Aidan, the quiet, sensitive young one who got the chair; and The Charmer. They were all mustering, for themselves and on other people's properties. They were staying in town for a while, a couple of months, till the season was finished. I called them the Gang of Four.

Tom and Aidan begged off; apparently Tom's fiancée was expecting them for dinner. 'You boys are shocking,' I said, 'It's already nearly midnight. You'd be dead if I was cooking.' They had an easy camaraderie, and a ranginess that only just concealed their humour. I realised it had been a while since I had relaxed.

'Nah. She'll be right,' Tom said as they pulled on their hats. I stood up as well.

'I should lock up the bar anyway.'

'And then what?' asked The Charmer.

'Then I get to sleep in the crappiest bed I have ever seen, with the desert wind whistling through the gaps in the floor.' I cleared their empty glasses. 'Thanks for the drink.' Always have the last word, I thought. Or was that flirting? I took their glasses and went back into the bar.

'Your shout next time,' yelled The Charmer.

'Only if you're really nice to me,' I yelled back. Definitely flirting. By both of us.

FIRST IMPRESSIONS #2

The town felt like another planet on my first morning. Or I felt like an alien. I went for a walk around. Saw all there was to see in about fifteen minutes. Noted where the police station was, where the health clinic was, what the café had on its menu (oysters — wonder how long they'd travelled to get here?). And counted the number of feral dogs around town — seventeen in all. I went back to the pub for a coffee with Sunny, who was holding the fort.

She didn't have any customers, except for Kurt and Sam, both drinking a polite and separate coffee. We all stared at the horizon out the entrance of the bar for a while.

'There's a meeting down at the hall this morning if you're interested, Blondie,' Kurt managed after a good twenty minutes. Words seemed to come out of Kurt either after thorough consideration or with much reticence. I wasn't sure which yet. 'Something about cattle. The Chief Minister's speaking.'

'Right. Sounds really interesting.' Sunny and I clinked our coffee mugs.

Just as I was venturing off to the community meeting, two men in ties came in. From social security in Katherine. In town for the day to check up on people. See whether their circumstances had changed. 'Where do most people hang out in town?' one of them asked.

Kurt was backing away, pretending he was deaf, and Sam looked instantly nervous. Sunny, attempting to hide her sarcasm, asked, 'Who are you after specifically?'

The guys shrugged. 'Anyone on social benefits.'

'Right' said Sunny. 'And you've tried their houses?'

One of the guys said, 'Well, not many have anything listed other than postboxes.'

'You new at this?' Sunny asked reassuringly.

The guys looked embarrassed. 'Yes. We haven't been to Mataranka before, so any insider knowledge you can give us would be most appreciated.'

'Right.' Sunny looked at me. 'What do you know, Pip? Any insider knowledge?'

I smiled. 'Nah. Got no ideas. No one declared their bank balances or living arrangements to me last night.' Kurt was now having a hard time keeping a straight face. 'Sorry, boys. You picked a bad day. We only started here last night.' Their eager faces fell.

'Hey,' I said, 'I'm off to a meeting right now, though. I'll pass the word around. You after blackfellas as well, I assume?' They nodded. 'I saw a few out this morning. Why don't you grab a coffee here and I'll send anyone I come across over to you.'

'That would be great. Thanks a lot. We appreciate it.'

Kurt's stifled laughter had become a coughing fit. 'You right, Kurt? Need a glass of water?' Sunny asked, as I turned and left the bar before I nearly wet myself.

I walked down towards the hall. I saw three Aboriginal people sitting outside the roadhouse. They were a young boy, an old man and a woman about my age. 'Morning,' they nodded. 'Hey. Two guys have just turned up at the pub from social security in Katherine. They're after anyone on benefits. I told them to have a coffee and I'd send people over to them. But why don't you guys spread the word and make sure no one goes to the pub for a few hours? I reckon they'll be there till at least lunch.'

They nodded. 'Thanks, sis. We'll make sure.'

I stopped in at the roadhouse. 'Morning. I'm new at the pub. Pip. How are you doing?'

'Fine thanks,' said the tight grey perm with middle-aged hips and pursed lips. Welcoming.

'Just thought I'd let you know that a couple of guys from social security are in the pub wanting to see anyone on benefits. Not sure if you know anyone that applies to, but if you could spread the word I'd appreciate it.' I wasn't entirely sold on her generosity of nature so I didn't go into specifics.

'Right you are.' There was a pause. 'Guess they'll be there for a few hours,' she offered.

'Probably at least till lunch I'd say.' I raised my hand in farewell and left the airconditioned bubble.

The community hall was a fairly new brick construction, which appeared to be rarely used. Inside there was a gathering of about 30 white people. A 40-something white man was talking up the front, standing on a chair — about Native Title, and stock routes, on Crown Land. Yep. Kurt was right. Something about cattle. And the white man speaking was the Territory's Chief Minister, Marshall Perron.

There wasn't much in-depth discussion. Cattle people asked questions about what would happen if Aboriginal people bought Elsey Station. Would they be able to erect fences to stop stock passage? And what about tourism operators? Would they still have access to the river for their cruises and fishing trips? It appeared to me to be just another politician working the crowd. I guessed this was community consultation.

I noticed that Tom, the redhead from the night before, was there with a girl. A thin, wiry, country girl, another flaming redhead. That would have to be the fiancée. 'Hey, Tom. How you doing?'

'Yeah good, Pip. This here is my girl, Jack.' His drawl was slow but warm with no signs of superficiality. And he hadn't called me Blondie.

'Hey, nice to meet you,' I said as I shook her hand. 'I heard they were late for dinner last night. I would have killed him if it was me.'

Jack was looking a bit confused. 'Pip's the new girl at the pub. That's why I was late last night.'

'Don't you go blaming it on me, mate. I was just serving the drinks.'

Jack laughed, thank God. Last thing I needed was a suspicious girlfriend.

'Where you from then, Pip?' she said in the loose accent of country New South Wales.

'From Sydney.'

'Wacky do. That's where I went to school. Haven't talked to a Sydneysider for ages.'

I smiled. 'Well, I'll be at the pub working tonight if you want to catch up on any gossip.'

'I might just do that.' I was smiling as I walked away. Wacky do.

GRASPING DESIRE

The second night behind the bar was much the same as the first. Just quieter. The four guys came in again — Jack with them. They sat outside and I stopped for a chat whenever I passed. Sunny came over and joined them as well. They were full of in-jokes and innuendos. Funny but painful after a while for an outsider. I could tell Sunny wasn't warming to them. She headed off to her room. The Charmer kept his eye on me most of the night.

Jack and I hit it off. Her droll manner and enthusiasm won me over. We reminisced about Sydney. About the beaches. About the busyness of the place. She'd been up here for almost two years. She hadn't been back to the city in all that time.

'Not many women round here to talk to, you know, Pip.'

I could imagine. We organised to have lunch the next day. At the café — as a treat.

She left not too long after, driving, even though she and Tom only lived around the corner. The guys left and the pub was quiet and empty by ten. I still had two more hours to go. By eleven-thirty, when Sam finally left the bar, I had made it through a chapter of *Anna Karenina*. While I was locking the front doors I heard a scuffle out in the garden. Shit. It better not be Sam. I finished slamming the bolts across and gingerly made my way towards the noise. The party lights were already out but the security lighting around the perimeter was on. Orange fluorescence throwing shadows around the tables. There was a guy sitting at the table nearest the door. Shit. 'You right, mate?' I heard myself ask, trying not to reveal my nervousness. At least it wasn't Sam with his unnerving, stewed bitterness after a few rums. I didn't feel comfortable around him.

'Hey, Blondie,' a smooth, low drawl. 'Or can I call you Pip?'

The Charmer. I relaxed. He was manageable. 'Shit, Lyell. You shouldn't be doing that to a girl.'

'What? Fancying her?'

Well at least I could give him points for pulling no punches. I tried really hard not to respond but it didn't work.

He chuckled. 'See, it's not all bad round here.' There was a pause. I was still standing on the step. Hadn't moved. 'So, young Pip. Have you seen the famous hot springs yet?'

'No, Lyell. I haven't.'

'Well if you hurry up I can take you there tonight. It's a fine night for a swim.'

I automatically looked up, only to see the corrugated plastic roof of the garden area. 'Well, I wouldn't know. I haven't seen the sky since four o'clock.'

He laughed. 'See, a girl needs to get out more and an outdoor adventure could be just the ticket.'

This was unbelievable. Second night in and already here was a guy propositioning me. And what's more I was enjoying it. In fact I was considering it. Seriously. 'Do I need to pick up anything from my room? Swimmers?'

'Nah. P'raps just a coat,' he paused to look at me, grinning, 'for afterwards.'

The hot springs are about fifteen minutes from town. Down the highway and left. We were sitting in the darkness of the cab of his standard-issue khaki Toyota ute, with only the headlights to mark our path. Feeling oddly safe. I didn't feel the need for conversation, or strange about being in his car, or even worried about his axe-murderer potential. Safe. I have always liked driving along Australian roads at night. Something about the expanse of wilderness around. The way it looks and feels completely different to daylight. And just how alone and isolated but connected you can feel as you travel through the darkness.

He didn't say much either. Kept grinning, though. I could see his teeth shining, reflecting the glow of the dashboard lights. 'These springs,' he said 'run constantly at 36 degrees Celsius. Right out of the ground. Really popular with the tourists. Good for your health some reckon.' Now he was being cheeky.

The springs were part of a tourist resort, a hotel and bar called the Mataranka Homestead. We pulled up and parked as close to the springs, and away from the main part of the hotel, as possible. I knew he had a girlfriend from that phone call the night before, and even though there only seemed to be a couple of other cars parked and no one else around, he was being careful. 'You'd be surprised how many people come here at night.' I could tell he'd done this before.

I climbed down from the ute and gently shut the door. The Charmer came round the back and stood beside me. 'This way.' He grabbed my hand and led me over to the sound of water. We rounded a bend in the path and I literally had to stop at the sight. There was a large, deep, clear body of water right in front of us. Slivers of steam glittered above it against the night shadows of tropical rainforest. It was magnificent.

I could hear a couple of voices up the other end and a dim security light offered some visibility. The Charmer leaned down and whispered, 'See, worth the ride.'

I smiled. 'Last one in is a rotten egg,' and I pushed past him and headed down to the water.

He slowly followed me. I didn't turn around but I could hear him on the path. I started to take my shirt off, then undid my skirt, stopping to pull it off. I stopped at the water's edge, kicking off my shoes and turning slightly to see where he was. He had stopped, his shirt unbuttoned, and was watching me. Bra and knickers? I wondered. What the hell. I haven't had a skinny dip for months. I was in the water in a second.

The Charmer laughed, his deep guffaw I would come to know well, then stripped off and joined me in the glorious heat of the springs. Day two in a new town, and most, if not all, of my moral code had been broken, even though, until I broke it, I hadn't realised I had one. But then, what is a moral code if it isn't constantly reassessed and redefined against the world?

680 KM NORTH-EAST

The difference between Halls Creek and Mataranka was remarkable. The land was different, more hills in Mataranka, and a brown chalky dust rather than that magic red of the Kimberley. There were huge bougainvillea and frangipani flowers and a tropical feel, but there was a drier look to much of the vegetation. Scrubby and untidy. The white people were stringier, leaner, as though life was harder. And even though it was more humid and seemed to have more water running through the region, the lorikeets gathered every dusk at the tap outside our house, fighting over the incessant drips in twittering billows of red and green. They never seemed to quench their thirst.

The Aboriginal people weren't as prominent. Not as much a part of the town as in Halls Creek. The town camp, used by Aboriginal people as a safe stopover coming in and out of south-east Arnhem Land, was just on the outskirts of Mataranka. At some point in the near past there had been a few small houses erected on the area for people to use. But the camp's electricity and water had been turned off and the walls removed from the houses so Aboriginal people wouldn't be encouraged to stop there permanently. Apparently no one had been paying the utility bills. Of course, Aboriginal people still stopped there, slept on exposed concrete, had fires and found water to drink, but at least the Territory wasn't paying for it.

And the police kept a real low profile. Almost as though they didn't want to know what went on. Almost as though they didn't mind what went on.

The kids on the streets were white not black. The black kids would be helping carry groceries to vehicles. Holding smaller babies, ready for adults to lift onto the back of trucks. They would be keen to keep moving. Mucking about in the dirt. The gravel. Eating chips. Drinking Coke. But never straying far from the truck. Or the adults.

The white kids hung about the roadhouse. Rode their bikes up and down the bitumen. Staring with wide eyes at everything. As though they had never seen what they were looking at before. Maybe they hadn't. I thought their fathers with squinting, sun-damaged eyes and their weathered, watchful mothers would generate surprise in anyone.

The whole population of the town moved and shifted depending on seasons, and family and government benefit days. Everyone trying to get somewhere else. There was a small group of permanent townspeople. Territorial. Defensive. Well, the women anyway. Okay. Not all the women. But a significant proportion were suspicious enough of two single girls to make it unpleasant. Make us wary.

Many people, black and white, came in off stations, off outstations, off Arnhem Land, or passed through, headed the other way — back into the desert. And all with an independence that ensured their distance. It wasn't an ungenerous town. Life just seemed harder. More fought-over. Fragile. Elsewhere.

The Stuart Highway is pretty much a dead straight line from Darwin to Alice Springs. The entrance to the bar looked east towards the horizon across the highway. The vehicles passing were a procession in homage to the combustion engine. Road trains, cars, caravans, police cars, trucks full of Aboriginal people, utes, vans, station wagons, Britz campervans, kombis. All at regular intervals. All at amazing speed.

When I started at the Old Elsey I thought the view looked the same. But gradually small differences began to reveal themselves. Changes. Shifts. From one day to the next. The growing density of the clouds far away on the scrubby, uneven horizon. The type of people who would stop on their way to Alice. Tourists in big campervans, talk full of crocodiles and Kakadu. People heading to Darwin. Territorians. On business. Running. Always leaving somewhere.

The time of the day brought different speeds. Slower in the morning. Faster at dusk and into the night. And each day punctuated by the Aboriginal liaison officer speeding past in the police truck and the same white guy from the lime-processing plant commenting, in the bar, 'Hey. Some darkie's stolen the cop car again' — and then cackling hysterically.

There were small changes in the glance of sunlight as it hit the oily bitumen at different times during the day. Sending rainbow reflections into the dim of the bar.

Each day always felt a bit different. Unsettled. Unsettling.

SUNNY DAYS AND THE KID

Sunny wasn't happy. She didn't like Mataranka with its intense insularity. With its almost complete absence of engagement with an outside world, unless it was emotional, irrational discussions about the unfairness of Native Title or all-round agreement that Ranger uranium mine should go back into production or tears at the demise of the buffalo.

The only person she spoke to, or liked, was Kurt. He had a life behind him and, as a Queenslander, hadn't always lived in the Territory or the town. He'd been a soldier in Vietnam, served in Korea for a short time, had two ex-wives and two sons, one from each marriage, and was the only guy we met in town who hadn't been charged with assault. And he passed no judgements on anyone. Unless they passed judgement on either Sunny or me. He was big on loyalty.

Even the 'big house', as it was referred to in snide asides, brought no sense of home for Sunny. It was the first house I had stayed in for almost a year and for Sunny it was closer to two. The 'big house' was a two-bedroom place with a large kitchen and lounge room, which sat on a square of concrete. The walls were all louvres and could be adjusted to catch the breeze. We had our own kitchen and even a little black-and-white television, so I thought it was pretty good, considering the circumstances. But the louvres also meant that anyone outside could move them to see in without really being noticed. The front step was in view of the bar, our travels noted in and out, and the neighbours (mainly Sam, Peter and Paula) took to wondering out loud to bars full of drunken miners and jackeroos where Pip, or was it Sunny, had headed off to at midnight last night. Or indeed who did Pip think she was, eating oysters in the café with Jack so soon after they had met. Gossip was flying thick and fast and we had nowhere to hide … a week in and Sunny was climbing the walls.

So, when the opportunity came up for her to go out to a station to be the cook, the only woman on the place, she leaped at it. Anything to get out of this black spot on the map. And while it would be the first time in six months that we would be away from each other, it felt like a good thing. She was going mad and I was completely distracted by The Charmer. That one night had turned into a full-blown affair — I wasn't minding Mataranka nearly so much. I was the one disappearing at midnight.

So three weeks in, on yet another clear, blue, sunny day, with just a hint of cloud on the horizon, Sunny packed up, got into yet another ute and left — for more remoteness, self-reliance and intensity.

I had the house to myself for a week (and much of the work) till they found someone new, a girl from Darwin, a Territorian. Karen. She knew a few people in town and Paula thought she'd be great.

PUMPING PETROL

The pub had a petrol pump as part of its service. While not the only one in town, it still did brisk business. I loved pumping petrol. Standing outside in the fresh air. Escaping from the bar. Quick chats with people. Talking about the weather. It broke up the monotony of a shift.

And all sorts of engines would speed, lurch or be pushed up to be filled. Fuming old cars on their last gasp. Kombi vans muttering. Motorbikes. Bullcatchers, the old cut-down four-wheel drives converted for mustering buffalo; and loads of khaki Toyota utes.

One afternoon I was in the bar, serving. The sound of a helicopter was awfully close. Must have landed somewhere near. The bar collectively wondered what might be going on. Then a guy, quite well spoken, leaned around the door. 'Any chance of fuel?'

'Sure. Be there in a sec.' I headed out the door, rounded the resplendent red bougainvillea and stopped.

'You can't be serious, mate. It's a helicopter.' And it was. A Robinson. A small mustering chopper. Clearly the one we had heard. The pilot had landed it across the highway. Just off the bitumen.

'She's fine. She'll take Super at a push. Although if you've got any AV gas that would be ace.' He looked at me hopefully.

I was stunned. 'Right. I'll check.' I went back into the bar. 'Any of you fellas got any AV gas stored away somewhere?' The seven drinkers all looked at me blankly. 'I didn't think so.'

'What do you need AV gas for, Pip?' Kurt asked.

'For the helicopter. But this mad bastard reckons it takes Super.'

Kurt was bug-eyed. 'Shit. I've heard of that but I've never seen it.' The bar was empty in two seconds flat.

'No AV gas, mate. But we've got plenty of Super.' The crowd was gathering around the helicopter now. Even though the pilot had managed to land it off the highway it was still mighty close to being collected at any given opportunity, by any given road train.

'Have you got one of the tanker hoses?' We did. Easy.

So we filled it. We blocked off the highway and made everybody stamp out their cigarettes thoroughly. (I mean really, this could blow us all sky high.) But it worked. I kept the gun of the bowser deep into the bigger hose, and the pilot kept the hose locked tight to the opening of the fuel tank. The crowd thought it was excellent. The kids were running riot and pretending to sniff the fuel. Even the roadhouse perm-of-a-woman had walked far enough out her door to watch.

After about fifteen minutes the pilot was sure he had enough fuel to get home. And hopefully not to have to tell any of his pilot mates he had run out of gas. We coiled up the hose and opened the highway again. Both the pilot and I smelt of petrol. That faintly high, intense, sexy smell. Difficult to remove.

He left after a beer, in a cloud of pale dry dust, but the story lived on.

THE GIRL ALONE

One mind-numbingly slow 33°C afternoon, an eighteen-wheeler Mack truck stopped right outside, barely slowed down really, and a young girl jumped out. The driver slammed into a higher gear and moved off. The girl was left in a cloud of dirt which lifted the skirt of her flimsy sundress, revealing her skinny brown legs and knickers to the bar. Well, really just to Kurt and me.

She picked up her one bag, an ex-army satchel, and crossed the highway, heading towards us. It was three-thirty. Her eyes adjusted to the dimness of the bar and she smiled. A broad, generous smile. 'Hiya. Wondering if I could get a glass of water.'

'Sure. With ice?'

Kurt was watching her. Not impressed.

'Ice would be great,' she said as she pulled up a stool close to Kurt and me. Kurt moved his stool away.

I put her drink down in front of her. 'Thanks.' There was silence, except for the repeat of *Gilligan's Island* on Imparja TV.

'So, where you heading?' My standard question.

'Alice. But I'm not in any hurry.' She was from the Top End, a Territorian, but I couldn't place her accent. She wasn't white. But her story wasn't only Aboriginal either.

Kurt skolled the rest of his beer. 'See ya, Pip.' Odd — he usually stayed till dinner.

So the girl, she must only have been sixteen or so, and I watched *Gilligan's Island*, the kids' shows and then the news. She avoided answering any questions I put about her life. By six o'clock she had nearly smoked all my cigarettes without buying one drink or ordering a meal. Clearly she had no money.

About five the bar gradually began to fill. A group of workers from the lime plant down the road rocked in. Not exactly endearing but usually offering some light relief. A couple of cowboys waiting to be picked up after a day of mustering sat outside the door. Two of the local women, the uptight one from the roadhouse and the girlfriend of a contractor living in town, sat in the garden. And Sam, Sam came in for his nightly rum.

The girl saw him sit down by himself, glancing around the bar, catching her eye, and she smiled. He smiled back. Now, Sam wasn't a looker. His bitterness seemed to soak through to the surface, leaving his skin white and insipid. He was slim to the point of skinny and without a breath of humour about him.

The girl sat straighter on her stool. Crossed her legs. Flicked her unwashed mop of hair. Puffed out her chest. She had no breasts to speak of and her dress was a thin piece of flowered fabric with spaghetti straps to hold it up. It sank into her waist and floated out from her hips. And while it wasn't new or very clean it didn't leave much to the imagination. Her body was young and unformed yet it was clear she was looking to tease.

Jan, the roadhouse woman, came to the side of the bar wanting another round. 'You shouldn't be serving trash like that in here, Pip. If Paula knew, she'd have you.'

I took her money and glanced up. 'I haven't served her, Jan.' I gave Jan change and her drinks and walked away to pour another round for the lime miners.

'What's up with her?' asked one of them. The nicest one in the group.

'Not sure. But it's the most she's said to me, apart from "two rums", the whole time I've been in town.' They cracked a laugh. And then they all checked out the girl, as if noticing her for the first time. There was something going on and I wasn't quite sure I was on top of it.

The girl moved. She stood up and leaned across the bar a little way to speak to Sam. 'Excuse me. Just wondering if I could bum a cigarette. I'm all out.' Even the cowboys at the door had turned to catch her movement.

Sam instantly became a gentleman. Pulled a cigarette out, handed it to her and then bent forward with his lighter. 'Sure. Not a problem.'

His drink was empty. As a rule we didn't speak much so I had taken to just filling it up when it was empty. Rum and Coke, no ice. I put a fresh drink down in front of him.

'Hey, wait a minute, Pip. What about you, young lady. Would you like a drink?'

She had settled back on her stool with the cigarette. Casually blowing smoke up to the ceiling as she arched her back. 'That would be great. Thanks. Bourbon and Coke if that's okay.' They both looked at me.

'It's okay if you have ID on you that says you're over eighteen.' I knew she wouldn't but I needed to make the point. At least for my sake. She slid off her stool and reached down for her bag. Dress riding up over her thighs and plunging down her chest. All eyes were on her. Her confidence was languid and expectant but also innocent.

'Sorry. I don't have a driver's licence. Just a library card. No age, sorry. But I am eighteen. Just finished high school in fact.'

Entirely made up. But what to do? 'Bourbon it is then.'

She moved her stool next to Sam's and smiled. 'Thanks, mate. That's very kind of you.' Her tone was almost prim.

Over the next few hours she made friends with the miners as well. They started buying her drinks instead of Sam. Sam was pissed off but what could he do? The miners were bigger, younger, better looking and had back-up. Even with the TV shrieking you could hear the lift in the atmosphere when he stormed out of the bar.

'Leila. Like Sheila but with an L' was playing them well. She was now the centre of the miners' attention. They'd moved to the wall at the end of the bar and she was holding court. 'Same again,' one of them said as I went past picking up glasses.

'Not for her. She's had enough.' She hadn't really but a thought had settled itself in the back of my mind and I didn't want her at any more of a disadvantage than she already was. The miners were all undercivilised anyway. 'And it might be your last round as well.'

By eleven the garden was empty except for a table of female

staff from the Homestead. I was out there cleaning up dirty ashtrays, half-drunk spirits, beer cans.

'Don't know how you work here, really,' came a slightly slurred voice from the table. 'The trash you have to put up with.'

I turned. 'Yes. It's really bad. Especially out here. Any old thing can get a drink.'

They heard me loud and clear. 'Oh. I didn't mean out here, honey. That piece of trash in there brings down the whole tone of the place.' It was the second time that day another woman had referred to the girl as trash.

'Yeah? I wouldn't have thought it could get much lower once you lot set foot in here.'

I went back into the bar thinking about how sharp my tongue had grown, how much like them I had become, and how infectious bitterness could be.

By now the miners and the girl were the only drinkers left. 'Excuse me. Where's the bathroom?' I nodded out to the garden area, glanced at the miners, grabbed a cloth and headed outside after her. 'It's here.' I pointed. The table of women had left. I picked up the glasses, wiped down the table, cleaned out the ashtray.

The toilet flushed. The girl came out. 'Hey. You okay for somewhere to sleep tonight?'

'Yes. I'm fine. Thanks for asking. One of the guys has a spare room.' The spare room would have to be bullshit if ever I had heard it.

'Right. Because if you weren't I could give you the keys to a room here. You wouldn't have to pay.' She hadn't expected that. She wasn't sure what to do.

'Well maybe that could be okay. A room here?'

I waved over in the direction of the demountables. 'Yep. In walking distance. Not luxury but yours for the night.' I realised she wasn't as drunk as I thought. Or as drunk as the miners. Smart.

'That would be great. Thanks. Thanks a lot.'

'Stay here. I'll just get you the key.'

Eleven-thirty. Last drinks. 'Okay, guys. Time to drink up. Got to close the bar.' The miners skolled the rest of their drinks quite obligingly. Surprising. 'Now, Leila,' I said as I ducked under the bar to shut the doors, 'You're right with your room?' The miners stopped. 'She's staying here tonight, boys, so off you go.' They all looked at each other. As though I had broken some agreement. 'Come on, guys. Out. Now.'

Leila scooped up her bag and gave them all a quick hug. Whispering in each ear. Her dress transparent as she passed into the night. The miners stood to leave. So long as they didn't start a fight I was happy. They stumbled out the door.

I got up early the next morning. Partly to get the room key back into the office before Karen saw I'd given it out. I went past the rooms on my way to the bar. Number 1 was locked. I couldn't see if she was still in there or not. Karen had the bar open already. Kurt was inside having coffee. No sign of Leila. Kurt gave me a look. What was that? I wondered.

I walked over to the bathroom to see if she was there. The shower was running. She came out, bag in hand, in the same dress. Slightly more dishevelled. Looking like the teenager she was. I couldn't help but wonder what her day was going to hold.

'Hi,' she said. 'You've been really kind. I'm just going to head off. I need to get moving. I didn't mean to stay the night anyway. Got to get to Alice.' She was fumbling in her bag for something. She pulled out a plastic purse and opened it. Two hundred dollars easy. In $50 notes. And then some $20 notes. She handed me one of them.

'For the cigarettes and the room. I appreciate it.'

I shook my head. She had obviously worked harder than me last night. 'No. You earned it, you keep it. And you'll probably need it.' I was angry now. At all of them. The miners. The fucking vicious women. At me. My naïvety.

She crossed the road. Stood in the sun watching for traffic. Any kind of vehicle. She wasn't scared. Full of the confidence of youth. But she didn't want to be in this place any more. I didn't blame her. Our small group, Kurt, Karen and I, watched her as she flagged down another eighteen-wheeler. Squealing his air brakes, blowing his horn, barely slowing, the driver opened his door. The last image I had of her was her boyish silhouette as the sun streamed through her gauzy dress. We heard her call out a greeting to the driver. And then she was gone. In a swirl of dust and crashing gears.

It was then I realised that out here, in Halls Creek, in Mataranka, throughout this remote land, I never really saw women by themselves. There would be the occasional trip to Katherine or drive back from a party, but on the whole they, we, were always in company. Whether it was other women or men. Always accompanied. Except for Leila. Like Sheila but with an L. Odd things happen out here. People disappear. No one to keep tabs on the invisible ones.

NIGGER

The clouds had started to gather on the eastern horizon every afternoon. Betting season had just begun. Betting on whether it would rain today or not. Aidan came in one afternoon when the air was thickening with the promise of water, and with him were two of his Aboriginal stockmen. He was building stock numbers and managing fence lines on a new station and had hired these two especially. Both about 25 years old, they were cattlemen with great reputations. Aidan was happy. And he treated them well — and paid them well — so they were happy too.

Aidan came round to the garden door and asked for three Emus. I took them outside and put them down on their table. 'Hey, Pip, this here is Thompson and Nigger.'

I nodded at them. 'Nice to meet you both,' I said, shaking their hands (something I had decided to take up as a habit months before in Halls Creek). There was a pause. And I just had to ask. 'Is your name really Nigger?'

'Yes, miss. Surely.'

I laughed. 'Well, you both have to call me Pip. But I can't call you Nigger. What's your real name?'

He was a bit confused. 'Nah, miss. My name's Nigger. Real.' Aidan was laughing. So was Thompson.

'Don't worry, Nig. She's just having a bad day.' Aidan nearly copped a backhander for that.

When I finished my shift I sat down with the boys. 'So tell me, mate,' addressing Nigger, with an arched eyebrow at Aidan, 'how did you come by your name?'

He smiled a big wide grin. 'Well, my father was the first one. He was Nigger before me. Out on the Roper. He gave it to me.'

I didn't believe him. 'Do you know any American history, Nigger?' Now Aidan was really laughing at me. 'Well,' I said imperiously, 'I just think you should know about your name. What it means to white people. How they'll judge you. Probably take the piss out of you.' Nigger was smiling at me. Thompson was trying to be polite. I sailed on regardless.

'In America in the sixties a whole movement started to give black Americans rights. One of the real insults that the black Americans hated was to be called "nigger". It's terribly rude to call any black person "nigger".'

'Yeah, but Pip,' at least he was using my name, 'it's my name.' The whole table erupted into high-pitched squealing and giggling. It was the biggest joke on earth that I thought Nigger's name was insulting to him.

'Right, well, just because you all think it's so bloody funny I am not going to call you Nigger. Ever. I'm going to call you Sir.' They thought this was even funnier. Aidan bought us a round of beers to calm us down. Nigger and Thompson had laughed so much they were crying. But I never did call him Nigger. Always Sir.

THREE DOG NIGHT

Tom and Jack went to Darwin for a dirty week. Not that Tom would say. Blushing was his main art form. They asked if I would mind their house while they were away. It was a demountable on a concrete slab on the southern edge of town. Just opposite the town camp. Sure. Nice for a change. The Charmer said he'd keep me company. Had to smile about that.

Jack's dogs were well fed and only barked on approach. Tom always hoped they'd get more aggressive, rather than hang back, but Jack couldn't see the point in turning an animal against its nature. These dogs, two kelpies and a staffie runt, were gentle but protective. They'd go anything if it was threatening and came close enough.

I had Tuesday night off. First night free in a while. Dusk. I sat on the step of the house in the gathering night. I could see the campfires just across the bitumen road. Could hear the voices, talking, laughing. Each side of that thin strip of bitumen a different language. A different world. I turned off all the lights and marvelled at the stars, nature's lightshow. The three dogs sat with me. Not quite calm. They could hear wild dogs, travelling in packs around town, roaming and calling in the dark.

The Charmer turned up. I was already through one bottle of red and opening the second. We sat out at the plastic table on the concrete, he demanding to turn the lights on and me not bothering to answer. Happy to be in each other's company. We went to bed. Hours later, must have been about two in the morning, he left. Back to his motel room to cover his (now) nightly foray. It was freezing outside. That desert night air could fool me still. I sat down with Jasper, one of the kelpies, who'd been a bit anxious all night. 'It's fine, girl. We're all okay.' Then I went back to bed.

But she didn't quieten. An hour later Jasper again, louder, more urgent. I pulled on jeans and a jumper before I went out. I flicked on the outside lights. The other two dogs, Cola and Ben, were down by the fence line, only twenty metres away but they weren't barking. They were just staring. Tense. Watching. Waiting maybe. Jasper was clearly the alarm and the other two were the security patrol. 'Okay. I'll just get a torch.' The two security guards waved their stiff tails in acknowledgement but didn't take their eyes off whatever they were watching.

I pulled boots on and grabbed a torch, locking the front door behind me. And then I stabbed the torch beam into the darkness beyond the dogs. I couldn't see anything, and turned off the outside lights and waited. Gradually, as my eyes adjusted to the starlight, my ears picked up an odd noise. Low moaning. Not consistent. Not musical. The camp. Shit. I took Ben with me while the other two stayed inside the gate. Ben stuck by my leg as I trained the torch beam in front of my feet.

Across the bitumen the moaning was louder. Out of nowhere came a stick of fire: a tree limb, burning and growing a life of its own, waving in front of me. I put my hand on Ben's shoulder. 'It's okay, Ben. It's okay.'

The Aboriginal woman, with beanie, boots and an old overcoat, dropped the branch and looked at me. 'You awright?'

'Yes. Me fine. You?' Pidgin was never my best language.

'Old one. She been bit. Bit bad. She over this way.'

I followed her over. Ben sticking by my side. There was an old Aboriginal woman lying down near the fire. The moaning had stopped. 'What happened?'

'Them dogs.'

I realised that the wound I was looking at was a dog bite. On the old lady's leg. The teeth had gone right through to the bone. And the bone was glowing white. Some blood, but nothing pumping. 'Right.'

No doctor in town. At this time in the morning Katherine Hospital, even though an hour away, was the only option — in Tom's ute. 'Katherine. I'll drive. You need to come.' She turned and said something in language.

Another woman, the same age, stepped out of the shadows. 'Me, missus. Me have to come too.'

'Right. I'll just get the ute. And some blankets.'

Without speed restrictions I made it to Katherine in forty-five minutes. A personal record. The beanie wearer sat in the cab of the ute with me. The other two were wrapped up tight and warm on the tray in the back. The glowing digital clock on the dashboard said 4.01 am.

At Emergency I carried the bitten woman into the fluorescent, gleaming, empty waiting room. The two old ladies gathered the blankets and spread them on the ground and I lay the woman down on them. Her eyes were open and shining, and she certainly wasn't complaining, but I had no idea what state she was in. The two ladies looked to me. I looked down the room to the nurses' station. No one there.

I walked the length of the room and called out. 'Hello. Is anyone on duty? We need help!' Nothing. I looked round the corner and could see two uniforms, standing just down the corridor. 'Excuse me!' An older nurse turned round and headed my way.

'Coming.' She quickened her step slightly. 'Yes. What can we do for you?'

'This woman has been bitten by a dog. I think she's in shock. She needs to be examined and looked after.' I hadn't realised I was panicking until that very moment. My voice was uneven.

The nurse had followed me down to where the women were. 'Right. And you are?'

'Me? I'm from Old Elsey. In Mataranka. It's probably been a good two hours since the bite. Look at her leg — it's massive.'

The nurse made a cursory check by lifting up the blanket. 'Right. I'll just get the doctor. We'll need you to stay though.' She hadn't even acknowledged the woman's friends. Hadn't even properly looked at the woman's wound.

'Do you need a hand to take her in? She's really light. I can carry her.'

'No, we'll be fine. Just wait here.'

She headed off back round the corner. I looked at the two other women. 'It's going to be okay. She's going to help your friend. I'm going to park the ute. I'll be back.' I remembered how much the whitefella sick house scares Aboriginal people. With good reason, I thought.

I went out and parked the ute. Probably took five minutes. I walked back in, not expecting the women to be still on the floor. But they were. 'Nurse come back?' I asked. The woman who had sat in the cab with me shook her head.

Okay, now I was angry as well as tired. Adrenalin was kicking in. I went down to the nurses' station and bellowed. 'We need to see a doctor NOW!' Nothing. 'Hey, nurse. Where are you? I need a doctor NOW!'

The nurse came back out. She said in a patronising manner, 'There is a queue. We are getting to them soon.'

'Well, soon isn't good enough for me or for them. You aren't busy. There is no queue. And I am going to stand here and scream until a doctor comes to see this woman.' She clearly didn't believe me. So I started to scream. In her face. Was it seconds? Maybe a minute?

A balding, pudgy older man in a white doctor's coat appeared, a steaming cup of tea in hand. 'Anything wrong, young lady?'

The woman was seen to. She even had her own cubicle. The other two ladies had cups of tea and biscuits and kept her company. And I stood over both the doctor and the nurse. Forty-seven stitches. Tetanus injection. Injections of antibiotics straight into her wound. A script for antibiotics. And her dry leprosy looked at. That's why she hadn't been in pain. She hadn't felt the bite initially. Hadn't realised a dog had bitten her. I think the moaning had been one of the other women. And I'd been right. There were no other emergency cases in the hospital. There had been no queue.

TROPPO

It was one of those stories I had been told but never quite believed. Going Troppo in the Top End. When the build-up of moisture in the air, the expectation of rain, of relief, and relief never coming, sends people over the edge. I had put it down as a myth, in the same category as the stories about escapes from saltwater-croc death rolls and the 'I caught the biggest barramundi in the world' tales. But gradually I realised it had some basis. Well, in Mataranka anyway.

I had thought that if you were a reasonable, sensible person, troppo madness would pass you by. It was only the absence of rain. Not a major health issue.

By now the afternoon betting had started to attract big money. It hadn't rained yet, which meant no one had won really. Those betting against it raining today were still suffering the effects of pent-up pressure. Those betting it would rain today were optimists or desperate. Or already mad. I could tell it wasn't going to rain for weeks. And really, I thought, all troppo season meant for me was more drinking, more fights and more trouble in the pub. The air was full of electricity. Tempers were short and people surly.

But with Sunny out of my everyday, I had lost my foil. My barometer. The person who kept me on the ground. Made me see straight. And, in truth, my temper was flaring and I was increasingly sullen. I was becoming ever more one-eyed. And cynical. I hadn't seen rain in months. Not since driving through the Kimberley when we had stopped the car on the road to appreciate rain on its bonnet and sun on its boot.

Drinking more and more rum. Watching the colour fade in the eastern sky from my front doorstep. Wondering at the way the lorikeets could hold on in any position as they strained and agitated for those drips of water. Thinking about what animals, and people, do to survive.

And I still thought I was coping — there was nothing troppo about me.

AFFAIRS

Maybe The Charmer was looking for a way out from his dusty, planned future. Or a diversion from the gathering storms. Maybe I was looking for something for myself. A secret. Or a safe place. It didn't matter. What we had was a connection. Instant and irrefutable. And the sex was great.

And while it lasted, the passion was a beautiful thing. The way he looked at me across a crowded room. The way he would leave the bar with his mates and then dash back for a secret kiss ('I've been wanting to do that all night'). The differences between us. His tired resignation about life ('my broken-down cowboy'). The way we would talk about betrayal and how people get hurt, and then how we would casually put those ideas aside. The way we would sit late at night arguing about politics and out of the blue he would say, 'You're gorgeous when you drink red wine, Pip' ('my Pip'). He knew I couldn't sustain my disapproval of his conservative views and he would wind me up just to see me double over with laughter, laughing at myself. Bloody hell.

The way I giggled like a fool. The way my heart sighed.

Of course I forgot that I could leave. I tried to imagine what it would be like to live up there. Permanently. What life would be like — with him. And he started to imagine what it would be like to leave. And we both knew it was never going to work for either of us.

But I did stay longer than I might have otherwise. The flame of desire meant I put up with the monotony of the days. The small-minded bar conversation. The crocodile tales and tears. The cussing and the name calling. The hot, moist, sun-filled days. It meant that all the plans about what to do next with my life included him.

And I think that as the air became thick and wet he just wanted a way out of everything. He just wanted to be caught. Which isn't to say that no one knew. Everyone knew we were having an affair. His mates. The punters at the bar. His parents. Even his girlfriend. Although she didn't know it was me. She thought it was someone out on a station. The Charmer told his girlfriend that it was Sunny. But perhaps he was desperate. Despairing. Wanting an excuse.

But the clear intensity of being with him is something I hold on to. The intimacy. The companionship of two people.

PROTECTION

Most afternoons a group of workers from the lime plant would come in. The plant ran 24 hours, so there was always someone knocking off. The work was filthy. Full of lime dust and dirt. And it was hard. But it paid well. The men who worked there weren't cowboys. They all had pasts and were either avoiding sending money to children, partners, mothers, or actively working to make money for children, partners or mothers. And on the whole they were great guys. Affectionately, and because everyone had to have a nickname, a place in the social system, called 'limers'.

But there is always one.

He had just started working at the plant and on his first visit to the pub he began very politely. Just sitting with his mates. Drinking. Then after a few drinks he started. 'Hey, Blondie. Hey, Blondie,' with a little hint of viciousness. 'Hey. You know you're pretty. Right. Real pretty. But you know what else? You're a snob.'

I hadn't really reacted at first but the word 'snob' caught my attention. 'Yeah, you're right mate, I am. And I don't have time to waste on you.'

The other limers thought this was great. A bit of a set-to. One of the nicest ones smiled and said, 'Joe, lay off. She'll not serve you another.' That threat was always there. And I had used it. Joe shook off the comment and kept going. Not addressing any comment directly to me but mouthing off loud enough for the whole bar to hear. Things I would do. What I would do them with. Me not being good enough to suck his cock.

'Right, that's it guys. You're all out. All of you.' The other limers began to object. 'No. He's pissed and I am not serving any of you again tonight. It's over. Leave.' There was always a momentary pause whenever I did this. No matter who the customer was or which bar it was, they always had to take a second to either decide to leave or risk real trouble. The limers decided to leave. 'Shit, Joe, you arsehole. It's still early, what the fuck are we going to do now?'

'Maybe the Homestead will serve you. I hear they're desperate for customers.' They left.

The next day I was cooking lunches. Karen was too hungover to deal with sizzling steaks and Paula was in Katherine. Karen called me to the bar. I walked out and there he was, Joe, the miner from last night.

'Hey, Pip. I'm sorry about what I said and did last night. Really. I am. I felt bad when the guys told me. I don't remember. You know, too pissed. So, sorry.'

I nodded. 'That's okay, Joe. Just don't let it happen a second time. Or I'll kick all of you out of the bar again.' He shook my hand and left.

Two nights afterwards Joe turned up again. He was later than the regular limers but sat down, ordered a feed and a round of drinks. The others were slightly cautious of him. I said hello, loudly, so everyone would hear. And we all settled into the rhythm of the evening. The Gang of Four came in, The Charmer darting those looks at me. Karen and her posse of female friends turned up. All a bit raucous but having a good time. And then Joe started in again.

The limers were all sitting at the right-hand end of the bar near the wall. This meant that to serve them I had to walk up to their alcove and lean across. And while I always had the bar between us, sometimes that corner made me feel as though I was boxed in. Joe was sitting on the edge of the group, closest to the other punters, and he started laughing about me. Talking loudly about my clothes, my legs, my hair. About what he'd like to do to me. If I wasn't such a stuck-up bitch. Amongst other things. He was getting out of hand.

'Right,' I said to the most regular and most decent of the limers, 'he stops or he leaves. I'm not serving him any more. This is no longer funny.' One of the miners got Joe to shut up.

The others looked like they wanted to disown him, and the Gang of Four, particularly The Charmer and Rob, were all watching intently. Fights broke out for no reason in this town and I knew that those two, at the very least, would see Joe as a reason. I didn't serve him again that night.

The next day Karen came looking for me. Joe had come back in to apologise again.

And so it went. Every couple of days. The limers came in. Joe would stay decent for much of it and then he would go off the handle. At me. I was getting really tired of it. Especially the apologies. And it still hadn't rained.

And then one night you could almost see the moisture in the air. The humidity was extreme. People were drinking more. XXXX, Emus and rum. Just knocking it back. The bar was louder. The swearing more comprehensive and the tension no longer hidden. Some cowboys, the Gang of Four included, were all sitting out the front, hoping for a cool breeze. The limers were inside, in the corner. Off-duty cops on the other side and a few tourists. The local women, some kind of girls' night out, were in the garden. And then Joe started. It was not the night to pick me.

'Right. I've had enough of you and your bullshit. You're not going to do this again.'

'Yeah, well, honey, why don't you kick me out? Yeah? Why don't you try it. Bitch.'

If I had been another five inches taller and male I would have jumped the bar and punched him senseless. As it was, all I did was tell him to pull his head in and that I wasn't serving him again tonight. The other limers were all bored with this game too.

I avoided them. I watched their drinks. Poured their rounds when their glasses were empty but kept away from that corner. And I didn't serve Joe. An hour passed. The limers needed another drink. I moved down and cleared their glasses as I went. Not looking at Joe at all. So I didn't see it coming. He grabbed my left arm. I think he was aiming to grab my T-shirt but he ended up with my arm in his hand.

I had a large, solid silver ring on the middle finger of my left hand. The way he held me meant I had a fulcrum to work against and, unconsciously, I simply added some force behind it. The ring and his jawbone collided.

It must have only taken seconds but I stood there looking, not quite realising what I had done, until the blood began to flow. Joe was as stunned as I was. The limers were shocked and the cops thought it was really funny.

'Right. Now you have to leave because you're bleeding. Guys, get him out of here.' They all looked at me. 'And I mean now.'

The bar had quietened. The Charmer and Rob came in with Tom and Aidan in tow. 'What the fuck …' The Charmer said.

Joe's blood had spilt onto his shirt, running down over his fingers, which were now clutching his jaw. He was looking at me as if I had two heads. The limers moved. They didn't want a fight with the local cowboys or the cops.

Early the next day Joe turned up at the pub, just after I had explained the incident to Peter, who really didn't approve of a woman hitting a man under any circumstances. Joe wanted to apologise again. He'd had ten stitches, and his face was swollen. Peter apologised for me — bastard — because I wasn't and wouldn't be sorry.

Joe stayed away from the pub for a good week. Then one Wednesday night he was back — in full glory. Stewing. With just one other limer. And yes, Peter made me serve him. I got him every second drink he asked for. Joe started in again. I just let him go. I stayed out in the garden area, stayed away from the bar. There weren't that many people inside. The Gang of Four came by. The Charmer completely offended that Peter had let Joe back in the bar. Angry. But I was past caring.

The boys left about eleven-thirty and the garden was empty shortly after. Just the two limers left in the bar. Shit. 'Right, guys, time to go. Pub's closing.'

'You shutting the factory on us, hey. Not what I've heard, Blondie.'

The Gang of Four moved back into the bar, the four of them standing watching, blocking the doorway. Ominous. I wouldn't want to take the four of them on.

'Hey, guys. These two are just leaving.' Joe and his mate turned around to see who I was talking to.

'Right you are,' said The Charmer.

Joe shot me a glance. Poisonous. But they both stood up. Finished their drinks. Turned and walked out the door. Joe said something over his shoulder but I didn't hear it. Didn't want to. The four boys followed them out and I slammed the doors. Locked them. Shut the bar. Set the alarm and went home for a long cool bath and a rum, no Coke.

I didn't see Joe again. A group of limers turned up a few days later. Friendly.

'How you going, guys?'

'Good, Pip. Good. How about you?'

'Hanging in there.' I took their money and turned to the till.

'So Joe, eh? He's gone back to Darwin.'

'Really? Because of me?' I was half laughing and the limers were in on the joke it seemed. They were all smirking.

'Paybacks, huh?' said one.

'What do you mean?'

'Well he couldn't work at the mine any more. Not with two broken arms. He had to go back to his missus. He'll be spewing.' I looked at them. Two broken arms? 'Don't worry, Pip. He was a nasty piece of work. None of us liked him much either.'

FRIENDS

When I was leaving Halls Creek I had written to Kim, the helicopter pilot. The letter wound up being ten pages long, not declaring undying love, but putting on paper my superficial attempt at understanding his loss, my hopes for him, and reminding him what a big heart he had and how life was to be lived. Wishing him well.

One slow afternoon in the Old Elsey, just as I had finished cooking yet another steak sandwich, I turned to the till and caught a glimpse of someone arriving. 'And what will it be for you ...?'

Kim was grinning at me. 'Well, little Pip. I heard you were here but I didn't believe it for a second. I'll have a rum if you're shouting.' I laughed out loud and ducked under the bar to hug him. It was great to see him. He grinned some more.

We caught up on all the gossip. Kept up a constant to-ing and fro-ing of questions and answers. Pete had a new girlfriend. Kim was seeing someone as well. He was spending some time with his family. Mustering work was quietening down for the season, with the wet not long away, so he had more time to himself. I told him about The Charmer. That Sunny was out on a station, not necessarily having a great time. I hadn't spoken to her in a while. The locals were fine and there was Sarah and Jim's wedding in a few weeks now. Something to look forward to.

And then I had to disappear to cook another steak sandwich. I came back and he was staring out the door of the bar at the horizon. Watching the light shimmer across the yellowed grasses, interrupted by road trains hurtling past his line of vision. He turned back to the bar and winked at me.

'Ten pages, huh Pip? Ten pages.'

I shrugged. Yep.

PEEPING TOM

Sam, the old guy who lived at the pub, and I didn't talk. It wasn't that we avoided each other, it was just that we had mutually agreed we didn't like each other. When Karen moved into the house and started to work at the pub, the two of them hit it off. She told him gossip. He told her gossip. Over coffee as she set up the bar in the mornings and over rums in the afternoons after she had knocked off.

And Karen was an interesting girl. She wasn't particularly smart but she wasn't dumb. She wasn't ugly but she wasn't a looker. And she wanted, needed the attention of men. So she went for anything. Anything that was male and breathing. And, to her credit, she was quite open about this. But in a town of a hundred or so, with few single men and suspicious women all around, perhaps being open about it wasn't such a good idea.

Anyway, Karen told Sam everything. I have no idea why. And he told everyone else. And I mean everyone else. He even told Karen's new best friend that Karen had tried to pick up her boyfriend. And while it was true, it was completely unnecessary for Sam to repeat it. He was a shit-stirrer.

But Karen kept on. With remarkable success. Two of the police (married), a visiting doctor, a couple of the staff from the Homestead, a few stray cowboys. Sam was loving it. He was living vicariously through her exploits. He needed to know the details, the dirt, the people and the positions. Too much for me. But he thrived on it. His beady black eyes would glow and his little pink tongue would appear through his beard and circle his mouth hungrily with each morsel of gossip.

After a couple of weeks living together, Karen and I started to feel as though we were being watched. Odd little noises when one of us was in the house by ourselves, watching Imparja on the television or cooking. Or sleeping. Day and night. Different times. I thought we were going mad, like everyone else in town. Karen thought her retribution was on its way and that a posse of women were circling the house, biding their time.

One night I shut the pub at midnight and walked the short distance to the house. All the lights were on. Blazing. I called out as I opened the door. 'Karen, are you okay?'

'That you, Pip?'

'Yes,' I said as I entered the lounge room, 'what's going on?' I stopped. Karen was kneeling on the floor holding a Smith & Wesson pistol. 'What the fuck!'

She lowered it. 'Man, I thought it was someone else.'

'And who would you be greeting with that?'

'Don't worry, it's not loaded. I haven't got any bullets yet. I just thought I would scare him. You know, make him stop.'

'Who? And stop what?'

'Sam. He's the one. He's the one who's been watching us.'

I looked at Karen. 'Are you sure? Sam?' There was something oddly right about what she was saying. 'That weasel.'

So we hatched a plan. We would stake him out while he was staking us out. We would have to catch him in the act to get Peter or Paula to listen to us. Even though I wasn't a fan of guns, we decided we had to use it. But no bullets.

It only took two nights of waiting. He was back. Creeping around the house. Coming onto the concrete path from the back, out of sight of the pub. No light that side. We had turned off all the internal lights except for a lamp in the lounge room and a reading lamp in each of our bedrooms. We were sitting in the bathroom waiting. We heard him, a slight scuff on the concrete. And then a faint squeak of the louvres. Outside the lounge room. I went out and stood in the hallway. He couldn't see me but I could hear him. He peeped through the louvres. And then he moved down the side of the house towards Karen's room, past the bathroom. We had decided that we needed to catch him red-handed.

We'd left the front door open ever so slightly so I could get out the door without a noise. The toilet flush was going to be the signal. It meant that Karen had heard him go past the bathroom and stop at her bedroom window. The toilet flushed. I was out the door in a flash. Quiet. Real quiet. I walked in bare feet round the side of the house and along the flat wall. My shadow was falling behind me. Perfect. I neared the corner. Karen was doing what we had agreed. She was walking back into her room and taking off her shirt. We figured Sam would want to stand still for that. And he did. He had his back to me, crouched low, his eyes level with Karen's bed.

I quietly put the nose of the pistol on the back of his neck. 'Hey, Sam. Funny finding you here.'

He turned his head slightly. Licked his lips and then a soft watery sound began. He was pissing himself.

We frogmarched him over to Peter and Paula's house. Loudly. So they would know something was going on. His shorts and sandals were wet with urine. He couldn't believe we had caught him. He was a sad mess.

He packed up his things and disappeared. No one knew where to.

I started to wonder about troppo season. About how much longer I could stay in this place. How much longer I should stay in this place. I mean, I had just used a gun to intimidate another person.

SUNDANCING KID

I had been hearing reports of Sunny since she had gone out to the station. And not all good. Just gossip but I was concerned, although I couldn't do anything about it. Not until she turned up. And then one afternoon she did. Didn't have long. They had been in Katherine all morning and they had to get back to the station by nightfall. Just stopped to say hello. She had four station boys with her. And they were boys. All of eighteen, if that. They sat in the bar drinking like maniacs while she and I caught up.

Actually, we didn't really have much to say. It was weird. Awkward. Almost like the light had faded from our friendship. As though it was the intensity and proximity that had formed our connection. Now she seemed absent. Preoccupied. And I had never known Sunny to be anything but present.

She kept an eye on the boys and asked really general questions. Yes, The Charmer was still a going affair. No, not much else was happening. I asked her about the station. But she didn't want to talk about it. We broached the subject of getting out. When we would. Where we would go. Sarah and Jim's wedding seemed as good an excuse as any. Really only a matter of weeks. Felt like a millennium away.

I finally had to ask the question. 'Sunny, are you all right?'

She looked at me. Perhaps for the first time. 'I'm fine, Pip. Really fine.'

'You seem subdued.'

'Just tired. Really tired. It's not much fun out there. Just work. And I have the boys to contend with.' There was a pause. The TV quietly filling in the tight silence.

The boys, pissed, started to wrestle out the front in the dust. For fun. She looked at me. Half smiled. 'There is one guy who's caught my attention but really that's just made it more complicated. You know.'

I didn't. I waited. She sighed. And I didn't know what questions to ask. (Still don't.) I just hung onto my belief that if she wanted to leave she could. That was our motto.

'Come on, boys,' she stood up. 'We've got to go if we're going to get home tonight.' She rounded them up like cows, or errant children, herding them into the truck. 'Hey, I'll write you a letter, Pip. I'll tell you about the station. About the boys. And hey. I'm looking forward to Darwin. Not long to go now. Just a few weeks.' It sounded as though she was trying to reassure herself.

A quick hug and she was gone. And I was left in the baking heat of a long afternoon. In tears.

The Sundancing Kid had disappeared. Her joy in living evaporated, drained from her body. In her place was a distant, faintly familiar shell. Another setting sun was casting shadows long over the highway. Like darkening bruises on the bitumen.

GUN DOGS

Wild dogs were causing problems in the town. Day and night. Children had been attacked. Older people harassed, and not just Aboriginal people. The shire decided to allow the shooting of these dogs if you were under threat. And the gun had become a bit of an issue after the night we caught Sam. I didn't want it in the house. Karen couldn't understand. 'It isn't loaded, so what does it matter?'

I said that people would always think it was loaded, and that it only ever made things worse. But now she was able to use the dog situation as an excuse. 'See, Pip, you never know. We might have to shoot a dog,' became her catchcry.

'Should probably start with the blokes you have sex with,' I would mutter.

The muster season was almost over. The stations were all preparing for the wet. Supplies were being ordered and picked up. The Charmer was back to spending more time in Katherine, where he had a house and a life, than out mustering or with me. The last of the tourists were passing through, mostly heading south.

One of Karen's friends, Mick, had been out mustering brumbies and had come back to town with six beautiful brumby foals. Their mothers had all been filed onto trucks and driven north to become dog meat. But the foals, too cute for words with their bandy, shaky legs and rough coats, Mick kept in the hope of producing some good stockhorses out of them. He needed somewhere to keep them for a few days until he was back from Katherine. We offered the yard, not big but adequate, behind our house. It was completely enclosed by post-and-rail fences and close to the house so we could feed them without too much trouble. And they were gorgeous, delicate, unformed things. Innocent.

So the foals became ours. We talked to them. Patted them if they would let us. Morning, noon and night. The kids from the town would also come down and watch. Want a go. 'Can I pat them, Pip?' Even old sourpuss, hurrumphing Kurt, found a soft spot for them and I'd find him in the afternoons leaning on the gate with his hand cupping one brown nose or another.

On the night of the fourth day of looking after them I was woken by screaming. It was an awful, terrified noise that didn't stop. The foals. Karen and I ran into the yard to find a pack of wild dogs savaging the foals.

The dogs had got under the fence and already had three foals down on the ground. Two clearly dead and the third barely twitching. One of the foals had escaped down the road with two dogs after it, and the rest of the pack, eight big dogs, had the other two foals cornered. This was the screaming. One of the foals, with the white in her eyes glowing from the moonlight, was screeching. A high-pitched, otherworldly cry of terror. The other foal was silent. His fear formed into a shaking that affected his whole body. Karen started to cry. And then ran back into the house. The screaming foal was trying to climb the fence backwards. The dogs were snarling. Waiting. In anticipation.

The garden tap and hose were round the front of the house. I turned the tap on and pulled the hose round the side of the house. It wouldn't quite reach but I aimed it high and used all the pressure I could get out of the tap. The stream of water was hitting and distracting the dogs closest to me. They turned and that's when Karen came charging back out. With her pistol. She trained the gun on the dogs without really aiming and fired. The noise was deafening. 'Bullets? You got bullets?' One of the dogs was hit and went down. The others only half noticed. They moved closer to the foals. I kept the water up and managed to distract a couple of them again. Karen fired a second time. 'Jesus. Aim at the dogs if you're going to use it,' I yelled as the bullet went over their heads. The foal was still screaming. Slicing her hindquarters on the fence in desperation.

'Here, let me,' Karen yelled as she grabbed the hose. She was taller than me and could get the water further.

I picked up the gun from where she had dropped it. 'You bastard dogs. Get away.' I had never fired a gun. Had no idea how to do it really, but I aimed low, level with the ground, and pulled the trigger. One of the larger dogs whimpered at the close roar of the pistol. It turned and left the pack. Limping in its hind quarters. I fired again. The dogs turned and looked in our direction.

Seeing a gap in the dogs' concentration, the silent foal leaped through them in a vain hope of escape. As he sailed through, tiny hooves collecting dogs noses and teeth, one of the dogs grabbed his back leg in its jaws and brought him down on the ground with a dull thud. The other dogs leaped on the foal. Tearing. Gutting. Ripping his throat open. His last attempt at a response became a bubble of blood. The screaming foal stopped screaming. She became very still and watched the dogs at their work. The sudden quiet was deafening and terrible. The tears were burning my face.

'Pip. What are you doing?' It was Kurt.

'Kurt. The foals. The foals.' He came up beside me and took the gun gently out of my hand. Then he trained it on the dogs and killed two, one bullet each.

'Bullets? Have you got more bullets?' Karen ran back inside. I looked at Kurt, a skinny-legged, sun-wrinkled old man standing in his boxer shorts, singlet and thongs. A hero. More bullets. He took aim and fired one bullet each into the backs of the heads of the remaining dogs. They all fell. As if in slow motion. Dead. All four of them.

The foal left in the yard, the one that had been screaming, looked to Kurt. Even in the bad combination of the moonlight and the porch light we could see the blood trickling out her nose. Fear does weird things to bodies. Kurt took aim and fired. The foal crumbled and was gone right before our eyes. Just a bag of bones left on the ground.

The other two dogs had brought down the escaped foal. Her guts were strewn across the street. A local guy had gone out and shot them, as well as two other town dogs that had turned up for the feast.

In daylight it looked like a massacre. Blood and guts from one end of the yard to the other. Six foals and twelve dogs dead. The shire came and took the carcasses. We hosed down the yard. Paula worked a double shift in the pub. And Kurt, Karen and I sat down for dinner, but we couldn't eat. Liquids. Just the hard stuff thanks.

FORECAST RAIN

The weather was on the move. The pressure from the north, across the Arafura and Timor seas, was building. The air was close. Sweat was a constant companion, and all living things were seeking shade. Refuge. Most often alone — away from endless small conversations and the minutiae of the days. Rain was forecast.

In the pub more loners were sitting staring at the horizon. Unaware they were waiting. For anything. More arguments. More hard drinking. More fights. And the fights between men took on a different complexion. Almost as though they were started simply to pass the time. Almost jovial in their enactment. Funny. But the women, the white women, started to really fight. There had always been the verbal assaults and threats, but in the heat and soaking humidity the fights became more physical. Vicious. And usually centred around a man.

For a small town there was a lot of violence. In the time I was there, a mere four months, there were a couple of suicides (white men shooting themselves) and a few shootings (arguments that got out of hand — best friends almost killing each other). There was domestic violence, assaults, property damage and threats. The town existed within a particular lawlessness. With renegade fearlessness — or perhaps helplessness — that rendered it outside the law. Not above it. Removed from it. Removed from the rest of, or even an idea of, society. The police presence felt tokenistic after Halls Creek.

I remembered I could leave. And as soon as that thought resurfaced in my mind, one softly hued dusk, I left. Emotionally, I was out of there. It only took a week to organise. Sunny and I spoke on the phone for the first time in a month. I told her what day I was leaving, with the plan of reaching Darwin just before the wedding; all she said was 'Right.'

The Charmer was disappointed and anxious but we figured out a letter system. I would write to him care of Jack and Tom, and he would come to Darwin to see me off — whenever that might be. And we rationalised my leaving and talked about him coming with me, but no hard and fast plans were made.

At the appointed hour on the appointed day, Sunny was waiting outside the house, ready for Kurt to drive us to Katherine. Kurt and I couldn't hide our relief at seeing her. Sunny and I couldn't hide our relief at leaving. We hugged Kurt tight and nearly fell off the step. Kurt was trying not to tear up. The three of us opened a UDL can of rum and Coke and toasted ourselves. It was only nine in the morning but it felt momentous and Kurt wasn't going to let us go without a last drink. We drank all the way north.

After the wedding, which of course was beautiful, and the rum-enhanced partying, Sunny and I headed east together. Me heading home, Sunny still travelling. Leaving Sarah, Jim, The Charmer and Kim at the airport, all awkward in each other's company. Sarah not able to acknowledge The Charmer — not able to look infidelity in the face. Kim and Jim full of jokes and silly handshakes. A little out of place.

Sunny. Adventurous. Enthusiastic. Game. Funny. Always a winner with the men. We partied hard. And worked hard. And we had amazing times. In our Australia. Talking long into the night about love and lost hearts. Driving. For hours and hours through the desert. And dreaming and planning. And laughing.

You can drive up the Stuart Highway from Mataranka to Darwin and believe that there is nothing out there. The forlorn trees and patchy scrub aren't pretty. Or inspiring. But to deny the unseen landscape, the vastness of the red unknown that looms in the back of our minds and presses against our nightmares, is to deny the majesty of the place. And the impermanence of white man's existence across this land. The Great Sandy Desert, the Gibson Desert, Balgo, Louisa Downs, Fitzroy Crossing, Warmun, Kununurra, Gordon Downs, Bedford Downs, Ruby Plains, Nicholson, Victoria River, Litchfield Falls, Batchelor, Arnhem Land, Borroloola and the Roper River all mean something different to me now. They all *mean* something to me now.

Do you know that if you stand with your back to a sunset, you can see the mirror image of the colours in the sky behind? It is as though turning away reveals the hidden miracle, the heart, of every sunset. In the desert the whole descending sky is a cavalcade of colour. If you only face the setting sun you miss out on reflection.

There was something about the distance, the harshness of the country, the small-mindedness and emptiness of the town, the loneliness, that forged deep friendships and intimacy very quickly. You found out people's true spirit sooner than you might otherwise, and you knew their boundaries well. It was hard to maintain over long distances. And even harder to replace.

Sunny and I remained friends, stayed in contact, for a year or so. Writing letters. From one side of Australia to the other. She managing another West Australian hotel. And another man. Saving to go overseas. Me working in Kempsey, a small country town in New South Wales. Writing letters to The Charmer. Receiving odd phone calls from odd phone boxes from odd places in the Territory, which would drag me out of a township existence back into the intensity of light and heat. Me, just kicking around, waiting.

Jack and Tom were married in 1991. I helped her find a seamstress in Sydney who could fix her mother's wedding dress to fit and I was one of the bridesmaids. It was a great wedding. Weird though. Surrounded by people from the Territory I hadn't seen in a year. In a dry, dusty country town in western New South Wales. Coming from my job at the ABC in humid Kempsey. All the guys, including The Charmer, dressed in black tie, the girls in light summer frocks. It all felt a little like Dimboola. Especially when the drinking and the fighting began in earnest. With the guys wrestling out the back in the dust, the Territory wasn't too far away.

I had nothing to say to The Charmer. We had last spoken a month before. He had called me to say he was getting married. To the girlfriend. I did understand but I still had nothing to say. Even though we wound up having to be in the bridal party together and had to sit through dinner side by side. It was the last time I saw him. I drank too much and took the best man back to my hotel room.

I stayed in touch with Sarah for the next couple of years or so. The infrequent phone call and letter. She and Jim had children, two girls, within the space of fourteen months. They went to live in outback Queensland where Jim had a job as manager of a station. Distance. Loneliness. Who really knows what the trigger was, but after two months he held her at gunpoint, out there in the middle of nowhere. She managed to ring her mother in Brisbane, who then called the police. She escaped with her life, her children and no permanent injuries — well, none obvious to the eye.

And Jim? He went back to the Territory, to Darwin, still working the cattle.

If I knew Jim at all, I knew he would be devastated. Dismayed. By his own actions. By destroying his family.

Then again, who knows what another person's life is?

THE RETURN

DISTANCE

In 1996 I was working in the restaurant of a cabaret place in Woolloomooloo. Shows every night. Big stars and performers just starting out.

One night, as the show played in the main room next door, I was in the front bar with Lenny, the bar manager, eating crème brûlée, drinking coffee and gossiping. There was a small television positioned right above the corner door so everyone in the front bar could see it. With the show on next door, the sound was low but I caught a glimpse of the late-night news.

I couldn't hear the words but I recognised the faces. The black faces all pushed up against the fence. I grabbed the remote and turned up the volume. It was Halls Creek. And it was a riot.

I was stunned. Transfixed. They were people I knew. That was where I had lived. And the footage looked as though it had been shot from inside the jail. The police had locked themselves in while Aboriginal people, mostly men, went on a rampage. The irony was disturbing. Distressing. And there were so many people. Hundreds it seemed. Running down the street in a cloud of dust.

Is that what it looked like from the outside? Was that the place I had lived? It was the same street. There were the same green street signs. The same bougainvillea on the side of the council building. But I couldn't place myself inside that frame.

I was shocked. Unsettled by the distance I had covered from there, from that time, to this moment in an Eastern Suburbs hotel in Sydney. Disturbed because I hadn't really thought about the reality of these people for so long, and if I did tell my desert stories it was as a badge of credibility, of one-upmanship. Competition. As proof that I was more authentic than anyone else in the room. Not as stories of people I loved and who loved me.

I wondered what had happened to make the town go off. What the police had done. Or not done. The brief news bulletin with the dramatic footage didn't explain. The blonde newsreader moved on to the weather.

But my demented imaginings, the memories from that desert, that time, kept haunting me. Did it all happen? Were those people real? Was I still sung — forever bound to those places and carrying those people with me? What was it, exactly, that I remembered?

Over the years, in different jobs, different relationships, different places, I realised that time had never left me.

I began to write my stories down, but really, to find out, I had to go back.

TO START WITH

These days it isn't so hard to track people down, or so I thought. I tried the *White Pages* for both Sarah and Sunny.

Sunny had one of the more common surnames listed for Western Australia and she had lived all over the State — impossible to track down unless I made 175 phone calls. She was from a big family and half of the people listed were probably related — so perhaps even with only one phone call I could have found her. It made me wonder just how badly I wanted to rekindle that connection. I Googled her but came back with precisely nothing that was even related to her, or the life I knew she had had. Sunny had avoided the eye of the twenty-first century.

Sarah had another common family name but I remembered one of her daughters' names, unusual with unusual spelling, and I Googled her. There she was, state athletics through her Queensland high school. I called the school and left a message for Sarah with my contact details. Nothing came back.

I Googled Jim — nothing. Perhaps the inroads of technology hadn't been as all-pervasive as I thought.

Next on the list, because I was avoiding The Charmer, was Kim, the helicopter pilot. I couldn't remember his last name so I called his old mustering company to see if they knew where he was, to see if anyone there remembered him.

An older male with a smooth, cigarette-laden voice answered the phone. I could almost hear the space of the remote station, the sound of the Victoria River, down the phone line.

'Right. You are out of touch, aren't you.' he said. 'He had his own company for a while, went bankrupt, went to jail in Darwin, joined a bikie gang there.'

There was a pause. I almost laughed down the phone. 'You're kidding, right?'

The heavy drawl came back and I could tell there was a smile there, a smirk. 'How long has it been, eh?' Another pause as the outback moved behind his intake of breath. He was serious.

'I see. Bankrupt, jailed, bikie. In that order, yeah?'

He laughed out loud this time. 'Yep. Pretty much.'

What do you say when the soft 22-year-old you knew is now believed to be a criminal? My curiosity wouldn't sit still. Why?

I Googled him and, sure enough, there were the details, or at least a trail of charges, of his deeds. Bankruptcy. Drug charges. The bikies.

I had a hard time reconciling the image of the good-natured, hungover helicopter pilot I had stuck in my head for fifteen years, with someone who had fallen so far out of society. How did he get from being that young, vulnerable, heart-broken boy to a man with the reputation of an outlaw?

I wondered, though, what he would say if I called him. If it was me? I got advice on how to approach a bikie gang from an ex-member and mentally reserved a day in Darwin to seek Kim out.

I went online to look for the Kimberley Hotel and the Old Elsey Inn. Both still in existence, although it seemed the Old Elsey was now called the Mataranka Hotel and Peter and Paula no longer owned it. The Kimberley Hotel was still owned by the same man.

I called Jack in Mataranka. Left a message. She called back and it was as though the intervening years hadn't happened. She told me about her daughter, Willow, how Tom was doing, how their Brahman stud was going. I told her I was coming up. To visit.

I tried to find a record of the dead Father. To see if anyone remembered him. Anyone I could talk to. No leads. No nothing. I called a couple of the communities he used to visit in the outlying areas of Halls Creek, but neither had any record of a member committing suicide in 1990. They offered suggestions of other people to call, retired ministers, heads of missions. Nothing. I tried Births, Deaths and Marriages in Western Australia. I didn't have enough information to track his death. I never knew his real name. I didn't know exactly where he died. I realised I knew almost nothing about him. And that feeling — the blank, empty feeling of guilt — washed over me again. The same as it did that day in the bar when Call-Me-Alex told me of his death. The cold dread that I didn't do enough.

I didn't call The Charmer.

GOING BACK

I hadn't really thought about turning up in Halls Creek at four-thirty in the morning. I had some vague idea that I would just hang out at the Poinciana Roadhouse till dawn and then trundle down to the hotel with my little red bag-on-wheels and extender handle. It was 2005 and the bus had pulled into town and off-loaded the mail at the new post office (clearly Australia Post had been upgrading its resources right across the Kimberley) then driven around the block to the Poinciana. I jumped out and suddenly remembered what 4.30 am in Halls Creek actually meant.

It was quiet. There was no one around, except for the Poinciana staff and a few Aboriginal people kicking up dust waiting for two of my fellow passengers. I was the only white person leaving the bus here.

It was too early for the sun to be seen in the eastern sky and my body remembered that this time of morning was the coldest. For a second, and it was only a moment, I felt worried for my safety. And then I just felt silly and old. Thirty-eight years old and here I was worried about rocking up to a roadhouse in the dark.

But then, as so often happens when you are travelling by yourself, the unexpected turned up. As I got my bag out from under the bus, a man, a white man, bearded and wiry and rugged up in a thermal coat, climbed out of a blue sedan parked near the petrol bowsers.

'You for the Kimberley Hotel?' he asked me.

I smiled and nodded. 'Are you here to pick me up?'

'Yes. I am.' I grinned and couldn't believe my good luck. 'It's no problem. We do it all the time.' Yes, I remembered now.

As he put my bag in the boot he introduced himself — 'Ken's my name.' He smiled through his beard and I realised he wasn't as old as I had first thought — he was, in fact, my age. 'Meant to pick up another girl, coming from Darwin. She was supposed to start work, in the restaurant, but she didn't turn up.'

'So not much changes,' I said.

'The story goes you were here a long while back.'

I nodded again. I wondered how he knew that — I dimly remembered mentioning it to the man who took my booking. '1990 in fact.'

'The town, it's bigger now,' he told me. 'We've got a new cop shop and an internet centre, and you wouldn't have had these.' With a flourish he handed me the electronic swipe card that was the key to my hotel room.

'Who uses the internet?' I asked. 'Tourists or locals?'

He smiled. 'Well, since the kids have been told they can't hang around in the centre during school hours any more, it's mostly tourists.'

We moved on to the weather for the remainder of the three-minute drive — while it had been winter cold over the last few weeks, the forecast was for unseasonably warm weather. 'You probably won't need that coat,' Ken said as he eyed off my black crushed-velvet coat with the big fake fur collar and cuffs.

He pulled into the same driveway that I used to walk in and out of fifteen years ago, and on first half-light sight the hotel looked exactly the same. The same old bougainvilleas leaning across the rooftops of the buildings, the same old signs at the end of the fence line towards the airstrip.

Ken parked outside my room — an end room on a donga, a demountable, impermanent structure that had lasted at least twenty years. It was one of the regular cleaning hassles for the house staff — a challenge even back then when the dongas were relatively new. Then they had warped carpet, badly tiled, paint-speckled bathrooms, and lifting fake wood panelling. Almost impossible to clean. Add to that noisy airconditioning (and I mean Mack-truck noisy) and I knew I was back in Halls Creek.

I carried my bag into the room and shut the door behind me.

SAME, SAME, BUT DIFFERENT

The morning light was the same honey wintery cool of the sun against the pale fragile blue of the sky that I remembered, but as I wandered around after washing the snoring and farting grime of long-distance bus travel off my skin, it felt warmer than I remembered for July. Humid even. I had never known it humid. It felt and looked as though a hot electrical storm was building over the West Kimberley and heading our way. I didn't remember this balmy summer weather in July. No chill off the desert this week.

Halls Creek looked as though it had changed. There were houses and office buildings in places where there used to be scratches of dirt and grass. The old cinema had been knocked down and replaced with a house and an alcohol centre (for the management of alcoholics). The police station was new; there was a new hospital next to the old hospital (almost finished but not quite). Construction had started on a swimming pool next door to the oval, which everyone was hoping would be open by the beginning of the wet that year. There was the telecentre with internet access; a new café; a new resource centre; new shire buildings; new tourist information centre; a new Aboriginal gallery and shop; and people seemed to water their gardens more than they did — the town seemed greener. There was kerbing and guttering works happening around the whole place — the beautification of Halls Creek was well underway.

But despite all these external changes, the town still felt slow, small, remote, with an undercurrent of anxiety — two societies, tourists and locals; two towns, black and white. And the highway still stretched through it, disappearing north and south. Distracting. Unsettling. Always somewhere else to go.

And the crows, the black, glossy, beady-eyed scavengers, still hung around in flocks, pecking at the metal covers on the rubbish bins, scrabbling at food scraps, watching for their next meal.

By 3 pm I had walked about the town too many times. I was exhausted. I headed for the pool and the bar. It was fifteen years since I was here and it hadn't changed a bit. The same square bar with corrugated-iron shutters and wood shutters; the same pool, with the addition of a sun protection cloth stretched over most of the water and outside dining area; the same barbecue rotunda; the same bougainvillea; the same palm trees; and the same high green fence with child-proof gates.

The hotel itself was under reconstruction. They had closed and knocked down the old saloon bar, my saloon bar, and only had the pool bar, the cocktail bar, and the front bar operating. It must have cut into profits. If you wanted a drink before 4 pm you had to go to the front bar, the pool bar wouldn't be open. It was hot enough to be swimming and sunbaking, and

I lazed by the pool, surreptitiously watching the comings and goings of staff and guests.

A couple of the younger staff were swimming, two guys and a girl, and I chatted with them about the pub. The staff appeared to be mainly transients with a couple of long-termers. All from somewhere else. The young girl, perhaps twenty years old, from Noosa, who had managed two years in the saloon bar and now the front bar, vaguely reminded me of myself at that age. She had had a hard night last night. There was trouble in the bar, fighting, one guy almost strangled, and five arrests. She nearly got punched in the face and wound up in tears once she had knocked off for the night. 'Drunk people really, that's all,' she said as she tried to understand why it got to her this time.

I decided I needed a drink myself (couldn't believe it had taken me this long) and headed down to the front bar. That hadn't changed either. Well, it had: it had slightly less 'cage' around the stainless-steel bar opening, and there were both pool cues and balls for punters to use on the table. The irony being they now called it the 'cage bar'. Apart from that, it didn't even look as though it had been cleaned in all those years. It had the same broken picnic tables out the front, the mangy trees, the filthy toilets and the smell. I had forgotten about the potent mix of sweat, dirt, unwashed bodies and the never-ending stench of alcohol being expirated from every pore. The renovation of the hotel apparently included knocking this concrete room down and erecting a sportsman's bar complete with TAB facilities. Beautification. And income.

I bought my gin and tonic UDLs from the twenty-year-old behind the bar, the same piece of stainless steel I used to work behind, and with a quick 'Sorry girls, I don't smoke' for the Aboriginal ladies coming in the gate — 'Hey, sis, you got a smoke, sis?' — I remembered that I used to smoke last time I was in this town. I headed back to the pool.

Four men and a thin, silent boy with big eyes entered the pool area. Two of the men were early thirties, one was the father of the boy, the other a traveller. Then there was the boy's grandfather, similarly silent, and another old man who just wanted to see the desert. All travelling together. Filthy after their drive down the Gibb River Road and then to Halls Creek. Their bodies covered in a thick coat of streaked grease and dust turned to muck by sweat. Stopping to fix vehicles at regular intervals and having just organised springs for one of their four-wheel drives to be delivered from Broome on the bus the next day, the two young men and the old man boasted of their adventures with relief. 'This man's been working like a dog. Like a dog,' said the old man as he pointed to the father of the boy.

They collapsed by the pool and the noise distracted all the other drinkers and sunbakers (all three of us) as their skylarking began. 'You can't get in that water, you're a filthy pig — you haven't had a shower in three weeks,' yelled the father. The other thirty-something laughed and dived headfirst into the cold blue water, not quite leaving a black smudge on the surface as he swam underwater to the other end. The boy smiled and slid in at the steps; his dad ran and jumped, throwing himself halfway across and landing in the water with a slap.

The old man, a voluble sheep farmer from regional Victoria who reminded me of a great-uncle of mine, with his farmer-rough hands and blotchy red marks on his balding scalp, was appalled by the fact that he had to go to the front bar to buy alcohol. He came back with an assortment of green cans and rum and Coke UDLs in plastic bags. 'Fucking animals down there,' he said. 'You wouldn't be seen dead in it.'

Later that night, I pulled up a stool to the pool bar in the half-welcoming light thrown from the square. The woman working behind the bar was a blonde 40-year-old, only two days in the job, chatty but not yet known enough or knowing enough to be smart-mouthed. She was from far western Queensland and spoke of skin names as she bought art from an Aboriginal man for half a case of beer.

Sitting at the bar, though, it seemed to me that some of the tribes were missing. There were no old prospectors leaning over the bar whispering about nuggets and dust. There were no cattle people, no stockmen or agents or TB officers or helicopter musterers. There were no hoary old outback men yarnin' up at the bar and cracking onto girls more than half their age. The fixed-wing pilots were still there, still slightly removed from the rest of the crowd; and there were still the contractors — the sparkies, the plumbers, the builders — but they hadn't been in town long and were loath to engage in conversation with anyone else.

Halls Creek felt an emptier place.

ABSENT GHOSTS

Second morning and I marvelled again at the light — the way it hadn't changed at all. The way it lifted the morning and flattened out the hills at midday, only to send the country crashing into those deep mauves, indigos and purples by late afternoon.

The new Tourist Information Centre was staffed by a white woman, large and breezy. ('We love it up here,' she exhaled, 'couldn't be happier. We're very happy chappies.') Her offsider was a young indigenous guy. I had seen him at the bar last night, slight and lean, with hair plastered down. I think he was the first black person I had seen employed by a non-black organisation. Although I guess the tourist centre is shire-run so it probably had some kind of affirmative-action policy in place.

I was the only customer this early and as I waited to buy postcards, the white woman gave instructions to the Aboriginal guy; her tone was sharp. He glanced at me before he answered her.

Hope, on reception at the Kimberley Language Resource Centre, was studying at Darwin University. Nineteen years old and a Halls Creek local, on holidays from university. She was three when I was up here and she remembered Matt who used to work at the centre. The centre itself was housed in a grand new building, and there were books and tapes and maps for sale. Clearly, it had grown, with an offshoot in Fitzroy as well. And that growth could be measured in tangible, purchasable product. From that bare room with those old people learning English and creating alphabets, there were now dictionaries, recordings of language, children's books, language maps with bright covers and drawings.

I met Hope's mother, Lucy, in the bar later that night. I had been sitting at the pool bar for about five hours, with Keith, the gardener, and Andy, a general handyman whose partner was a teacher out at Balgo, an Aboriginal community 350 kilometres south-west of Halls Creek. We'd been talking about the town, the petrol sniffing out at Balgo — how the cops believed they had it under control with the help of Opal petrol, fuel that doesn't give a 'high'. And the rodeo coming up in a couple of weeks — and the fact that I would miss it.

A thin Aboriginal woman, probably no older than me, but looking older, with straight brown hair, dusky brown skin and an attention-grabbing swagger, walked into the bar. She was drunk and started mouthing off at three white boys, contractors sitting on the other side of the bar, because they wouldn't talk to her. 'What, you think I'm stupid? I've got a degree in linguistics. My daughter Hope, she's studying medicine in Darwin. Not blackfella medicine. Your medicine, proper medicine. She's going to be a doctor. And what are you?' The three men didn't know what to do or say. They just wanted her to shut up and leave.

'Hey,' I said. 'I met Hope today at the language centre. She's great. She's on holidays, hey.'

Lucy looked at me and stopped yelling. My drinking partners looked at me in surprise — they had had run-ins with Lucy before and, while admitting she was 'really smart', they could write a long, long list of her transgressions when she was drunk.

Lucy smiled, 'Yeah, she's beautiful. She's going to be a doctor.'

'I know, she told me. You must be really proud of her.'

'Yes. She's up in Darwin. She's going to be a doctor. But these dickheads here, these blokes they won't even talk to me. What, you think I'm just another drunk black woman, hey?' She turned back to yell at them again. At any moment she was going to be ejected. But after one more rant at the white men she left of her own accord.

The next morning, as I wandered about town taking photos, I saw Lucy leaning face down on the bowed fence of the arts centre. Head on her folded arms, her body was flattened against the chicken-wire fence in an alcohol-induced rest in the early sun.

I headed down to the new cop shop and asked the plump blonde woman on the desk, not in uniform, if I could speak to the officer in charge. While we waited for him to come out I explained why I was in town. She told me she was the senior sergeant's wife and that they had recently moved back here after being away for many years.

'What do you think has changed about the town?' I asked.

'You know what, Pip,' she said as she leaned across the counter towards me, almost whispering conspiratorially, 'it's greener. I don't remember it being so green. People seem to water their gardens more, take more pride in them.' I nodded and agreed. Although this was only in the white part of town, the bits the tourists saw.

The senior sergeant came out and let me through the security-coded door into the back of the building. He was a sergeant in Halls Creek back in 1990 and had recently been promoted back to the station. I didn't remember him and he didn't remember me, but we both agreed that we had had fun back then. Not quite the same now, apparently; no more staffies for on-duty cops, that's for sure.

I asked him what the difference was for him, and he started by describing Halls Creek as an Aboriginal community — something none of the cops would have done fifteen years ago.

He talked about cracking down on street drinking and working with the shire to decrease the level of rubbish around town. I asked about the 1996 riot, the one I had seen on television, and he was, understandably, a little evasive. He wasn't here then and he had new staff, young guys all keen to be good police officers — not from an older generation or with that 'cop' attitude many locals were so wary of — but he did say that it came down to individual police, 'whoever is passing through'.

The new lock-up was opened in 1993. 'Always on the cards' was the answer when I asked whether this had had anything to do with the recommendations from the Royal Commission into Aboriginal Deaths in Custody. It didn't really look anything like the old one — all steel and smooth edges —

except for the perimeter fencing. I laughed about the time I was locked up. He laughed but didn't remember. But then it wasn't him who locked us up.

As we walked back from the lock-up the senior sergeant showed me a wall of photos; the second along was the force from 1990. They were standing in a row in their brown uniforms. Most of the faces I recognised. The senior sergeant filled me in on where they all were. One had died of a massive heart attack; two others were out of the job — one with family problems and the other 'got into some trouble with a girl from the pub' in Halls Creek. All the others were still policemen in Western Australia.

I asked about the suicide of the Father. He couldn't help me. Didn't remember him or his death.

We shook hands and I let myself out through the flash security door, back into the harsh mid-morning sun and tourist traffic on the highway.

If I had come back to town looking for ghosts — they weren't there.

HELL'S CRACK

Groups of Aboriginal people, all shapes and ages, walked the streets, heading somewhere, shopping, hanging out, in Snoop Doggy Dog T-shirts and gangsta clothes, huge high-top sneakers and caps of all descriptions. Way cool. Cars full to overflowing with black faces and arms squeezing out of windows. Kids packed to the roof racks and red dust lathered over everything. Stringy, gangly cowboys waking up in the shade of the gums in the park after a big night, still with their hats wedged firmly on their heads, a fine layer of red dust turning their black skin a burnished brown. Boys on bicycles riding in small groups around the town. Women coming out of supermarkets (now there were three, plus a Coles Express and a liquor shop) with mounds of plastic bags marooning them on the concrete footpaths as they waited for a lift. Pint-sized girls in pink pants and bare feet, wearing attitude like a third arm, sucking on icy poles and glancing back at me as they passed.

I was on the way back to the pub. I stopped in at the butcher's. Jamie Savage was a little man with a great sense of humour — he hadn't changed his business cards in fifteen years:

Lorraine & Jamie Savage of
Halls Creek Meat Supply Welcome You,
and with typical Kimberley sincerity …
We offer Tough, Tasteless, Fatty Meat & 'Iffy Seafood',
at City prices plus freight etc. etc. etc.

I asked Jamie whether he knew anything of the whereabouts of Jean-Paul. He did. 'He left town over a year ago now. Went back to Perth. Retired down there. The guy who owns the liquor shop will know exactly where — he was working for them once he gave up hairdressing.'

The liquor shop sits at the Kununurra end of the town, and from the outside looks like a large corrugated-iron shed. I walked into a fluorescent-lit almost empty shop. The ceiling-to-floor fridges around the walls were oddly bare. I explained to the man behind the counter that I was wondering about Jean-Paul. That I knew him fifteen years ago.

The man smiled. 'Yes. Jean-Paul. He only left town eighteen months ago. He stopped hairdressing and worked for us for the last eight years, here in the bottle shop. One of his friends, though, got really ill. When she died I think it gave him a jolt and he decided to retire. To have an easier life for a bit. Look after himself.'

I laughed. 'Bet he's still drinking his cocktails down there though.'

'Yes. Although he did become pretty much a champagne man over the last few years. He'll be lolling around on a couch, sipping away. He calls every six months or so for a chat. Talks to the wife mostly but, yeah, he stays in touch.'

'Next time he calls, can you let him know that Pip said hello. He may not remember me — I used to have blonde hair — Blondie was my nickname. Pass on my best wishes.'

'Not a problem, love.'

I left the alien white light for the midday sun. And the pub.

I sunbaked and drank gin, reading as I half listened to the four men from yesterday talking about the problems with their vehicles, as the boy sat and ate his chips in silence. It was Friday afternoon and everyone was gradually turning up at the bar ready for a night. The contractors were showered, their wet hair combed flat, and drinking at the pool bar. The tourists, older men and women with Velcro sandals, and the younger ones with thongs, shorts and short, short skirts sat at the round tables near the pool. The travelling health-and-welfare workers in their groups of four or five ordered big meals and drank cocktails, garrulous, at the edge of the light thrown from the bar. The locals, a white woman, a black woman and the guy from the Tourist Information Centre, sat on one side of the pool bar, with one of the staff, the girl who nearly had her face punched the night before, now on her night off.

Me? I sat at the bar with Keith. He fancied me but he also just fancied a chat and a drink with a new face, so I thought I was fairly safe. Although after four hours of hard drinking, what is safe? I learned quite a lot about him. His dad's death, his ex-wife, his kids, his friend's suicide. And he found out bits about me. This remote desert throws unlikely people together and they make the best of what is offered. This touchstone, this intensity behind the surface of the town, hadn't changed.

The old sheep farmer sat with us from time to time, conscious of wanting company but not wanting to disturb us. He was, for all his brashness, a lovely man. His wife was looking after the sheep while he was away, and although he had been making ribald comments about some of the women in the bar throughout the night, when he started to tell the story of how he had left her to the lambing while he took the opportunity of a lifetime to go through the desert, his eyes misted over.

'I tried to tell her, you see, before I left, that some of them wouldn't be born right. You know, there's always a couple that, you know, for whatever reason, won't live. She's never had to do that, you know, kill a newborn lamb, and she said she wouldn't, that there was no way, that she'd raise them herself — all that palaver. But, you know, Pip, I spoke to her the other night and she said, "Love, I did it, I couldn't let it live. I did it just as you said. The poor thing wasn't right, not like the others." A man couldn't ask for a better woman.'

His arthritic knees were playing up because of all the bumps and thumps travelling down the dirt highways, and he was a bit wobbly on his pins from all the OP rum he was drinking. He misplaced his hat and began to sing choruses of shearing songs — in full voice and full filthy vocabulary. The whole bar was laughing, and this 70-plus man, larger than life and missing his wife, could have gone all night.

Keith and Andy were calling Halls Creek Hell's Crack. I hadn't heard that before.

'THE RESORT'

Standing in front of one of the supermarkets — the one with the only working ATM in town since the Coles Express one died — I marvelled at the level of security required to run a shop in this place. The door was a gap in the full corrugated iron front wall of the shop. There was a padlock and chain used to secure the sliding fencing that formed the outer perimeter of the business. There were no windows and no light (apart from fluorescent) inside the shop. And even the ATM was chained down with just enough links so it could be dragged back inside each evening at closing time.

The machine whirred away as it accepted my card; I punched in the numbers and nothing happened. That ominous electronic message flashed on the dirty screen: *Please check with your card issuer. Your card has been retained.*

I was on the main drag of this dusty, hot, bedraggled town and I had no way out. My life disappeared before my eyes and I felt 23 years old again. I now had no credit card and no way of paying for the hotel, or the bus trip to Katherine — no way out. At least not until I could call the bank (it was Saturday, and already 6 pm in Sydney) and sort something out.

My panic rose — panic I didn't know I had. What if I had to wait till Monday? What if I couldn't leave even then? What if I got stuck in Halls Creek? Sweat started to gather under my arms and in the small of my back. My breath shortened. I felt ill. I began to work through the list of people I could call to lend me some money until I got a new card. I almost cried.

Then as I walked back to the hotel, because I didn't know what else to do in this town, it dawned on me that I had another credit card — my work's corporate American Express. The relief was a force of nature all of itself. My body released the pent-up emotion and I found myself, fifteen years on, once again running and screaming down Roberta Avenue towards the hotel, ready to leave this place again. There was nothing to keep me here. I could move on.

I stopped at the brand-new café near the Tourist Information Centre for a steak sandwich and sat out the front at the green plastic tables near the statue of Russian Jack, the man who pushed an injured gold prospector in a wheelbarrow the fourteen kilometres from Old Halls Creek into the new town for medical treatment.

The only other customers were a white woman, her Aboriginal husband and their three children. They sat and laughed and ate their hamburgers. The man was big and solid, wearing the clothes of a contractor: blue work shirt, blue jeans and big yellow-brown lace-up work boots. His wife had the look of a tired mother of three children under four years old, but she still managed to smile and laugh at her husband's comments. The kids were funny; the two girls were trying to escape their dad; he pretended not to notice them and then just as they put their feet over the edge of the verandah he roared like a lion and dived for them. The mother had her baby son on her knees and he clapped his hands at his father's game. Much giggling and hugging followed.

As I sat there, with barbecue sauce dripping out of my slices of white bread and between my fingers, I realised that I had never seen this level of inter-racial relationship before in Halls Creek. There were always relationships between white men–black women and black men–white women, but I didn't know of any that were this open, this public, this tangible. There was another round of screaming from the girls and the five of them descended into giggles again.

When I got back to the hotel it was still early, so Keith and I headed to the cage bar for a drink. There were a couple of people playing pool on the table inside. One of them, a young *gadiya* woman with long hair and jeans, was a teacher. I got the full rundown of her sexual history from Keith, as we stood and drank our UDLs by the wall in the front outdoor section. I didn't get her name.

While we were there, Keith agreed to buy a piece of art, an eagle head painted over a landscape, for a case of beer. About $40 in Halls Creek. The two Aboriginal guys, the artists, were also trying to get him to buy some spears, but he wanted them 'painted up', and the ones they had with them were just a plain, dull red.

'Paint them tomorrow, when you're sober, mate. Not now. I don't want you to paint them when you're drunk, all right?' The two artists nodded as they took the case of beer, calling as they went, and a rough-and-ready crowd of blackfellas formed a parade after them as they headed for the dinner camp across the road.

I met Jodie in the pool bar later. She was Andy's girlfriend, the teacher out at Balgo. She called Halls Creek 'The Resort' — with clear irony. It had been used on some advertising for the hotel at some point and she hadn't forgotten it. She often came in for weekends with Andy, a three-hour drive each way over isolated dirt roads.

Jodie asked me when I was leaving ('Because everybody does, honey') and I explained that I was booked on a bus out of town on Monday morning. Jodie was driving to Alice Springs the next day. She asked whether I wanted to keep her company on her trek down the Tanami Highway. She could tell I was tempted. 'You don't have to decide now — I'm leaving about 10 am tomorrow so if you want to come, come — just knock on my door in the morning.'

If I could still make Katherine in time to meet up with Jack and Tom, then why not? I changed my bookings with the bus company.

As I walked across the car park the next day, a crisp, clear, sunny morning, the crows were already circling over the town, and the sounds of travellers packing vehicles, that low murmur of excitement as they called to each other, was burbling throughout the hotel.

I knocked on Jodie's door.

'So you're on, then?' she said through a yawn. 'I'll be ready by ten.'

I took a last walk around Halls Creek, this town that had lived within me for so many years. I took photos of the same view, unchanged after all this time. The same beer advertising signs, only more faded and with more graffiti. The same red roads with slightly more kerbing. It was early and the sun, coming up over the Great Northern Highway, was just high enough to skate across the treetops and cast a glare off the bitumen road. The road looked like black glass, as though it had just rained. The sky was a tourmaline blue. Hard and clear as though it could crack.

I felt odd about not getting the bus across the north-east Kimberley and into the Territory, about not finishing the trip as I meant to, but mostly I just felt the pleasure in moving on.

I was once again excited to be leaving Halls Creek.

'ALICE SPRINGS 1554 KM'

The road sign, as we turned off the Great Northern Highway onto the Tanami Highway read: 'ALICE SPRINGS 1554 KM'. But it was about 300 kilometres to Balgo — our first stop.

Enclosed in the humidicrib of a car jam-packed with stuff — bottles of whisky (for other staff at Balgo, even though it is a dry community), boxes of UDLs, slabs of soft drink, contact-lens medicines, hair dye, empty cardboard tubes for blank canvas to be rolled into, and suitcases — we hurtled down the road and talked about life. The bitumen soon disappeared into red dirt, with the tread marks of other cars and trucks leading our way through the very spine of Australia. South, through the red, dusty desert.

We turned off the Tanami to Balgo. Balgo is a very remote and beautiful place. As you drive into the community you have to pass between two hills, swathes of red and purple rock spun around and around, which simply appear out of nowhere. One minute the horizon is flat, never-ending, sweeping across the land, and the next there are the hills.

The signs on the side of the road as we drove into the community all said that you needed to be using Opal fuel. Jodie's 4WD Subaru still ran on unleaded fuel, and she told me a story of how she had locked herself out of her fenced house one night after driving back from Halls Creek. She had to stay outside the fence all night and the kids kept trying to steal the fuel in her tank. She took to lying underneath the car, setting off the alarm whenever they crept close.

Petrol sniffing in Balgo was more under control now than it had been in the past, although Jodie talked about it going in cycles, and while the Opal roll-out had been invested in by the government there didn't seem to be much incentive for tourists or rental companies or even locals to swap their cars over.

Jodie also told me that grapes cost $22.95 here. I asked why they were so expensive; after all, we were only three hours out of Halls Creek where they were only $4.95 a kilo. Jodie wasn't sure; all she knew was that she, and the rest of the community, had to pay the price for living out there.

We drove to her prefab house, one of the many, all alike, with huge fences and padlocked gates and perimeter lighting. There we unpacked and repacked the car for the trip to Alice.

We took her dog and two cats with us, loose in the back. I had never seen anything like it. The cats just curled up in corners amongst the luggage, and Jimmy, the dog, clambered over the bags so he sat in between our two front seats, his head level with our shoulders. They didn't move for most of the trip, although one of them farted ruthlessly.

We watched the sign marking the border between Western Australia and the Northern Territory as we pelted towards it, glistening in the sun, hard, man-made in a landscape full of softer edges and rolling horizons.

As the day stretched into a long, hazy dusk, Jodie started to drive slowly and more carefully. 'Too many animals out here at night.' Just then a feral cat leaped onto the road and darted across the red dirt in front of us. It was huge. As big as a dog, a retriever-sized dog. Neither of us could believe it.

'Imagine meeting that when you're camping,' Jodie said. I shivered and hoped we wouldn't — camp or meet a wild cat.

Rabbit Flat is referred to as 'the remotest roadhouse' in Australia and is, quite literally, a square building right in the middle of the continent.

We pulled up at the petrol pump, a distance from the roadhouse, and Jodie headed inside, to find the owner's wife, Jacquie. She was French and still retained a thick accent even though she had been in Australia, and out here in this place of flat vowels, for over 40 years.

After filling the tank, we drove the car up closer to the roadhouse and parked it so we could see all comers from the inside. I headed to the bar for food. The feel of the roadhouse was almost Mediterranean, with shutters on each window (no glass) of the covered café area. Inside the squat, murky mustard-brown building the walls and floors were covered in murals — snakes, roads, tussocky hills, stringy trees, the red expanse — renditions of the now dark land just outside the door. It was also dark inside the café, I assumed because it gets so hot and so cold out here. The dimly lit square was probably a refuge from both. The bar heaters were already on when we arrived at five o'clock but the room was still chilly.

The 'bar' was a serving hatch stuck into a section of the wall at the back of the room, with wire mesh anchored firmly all around it. The signs were all handwritten and weathered yellow with age. The only alcohol on offer was beer. Spirits had been stopped since the drinking crowd got too rowdy and, with only Bruce, the owner, to sort them out, too unmanageable and dangerous.

There was an Aboriginal family ordering food. Bruce, behind the hole in the wall, was carefully taking their orders, asking them for their names (so he remembered who had what) and taking their money. He did all of this respectfully and without any hint of judgement, and not once was there even a glance my way, the suggestion that a white person would get served first, or even a comment thrown to the only other whitey in the room.

It seemed such a little thing but I found it extraordinary. In all other places — bars, restaurants, cafés, shops, roadhouses, now or fifteen years ago — I would have at least been referred to, nodded at ('Be with you in a minute'), over and above any black people already waiting. I remember back in the pub when I used to make *gadiyas* wait their turn and they would hassle me for it. And at the roadhouse in Halls Creek when I was told to serve the 'white folks first'.

I wondered who this grey-haired, headband-wearing, calm man was. Who his French wife was. How did they end up in this place?

After dinner I was struck quiet with tiredness and the realisation of just how far removed we were from anyone, anything. The star-filled sky shimmered in some unfathomable rhythm, and the desert wind felt gentle, lilting, but soon whipped across the flat plains and chilled to the bone. I wished for the generator to be turned off so that the peace of the desert could prevail but the mechanical hum and rumble continued throughout the night.

We gathered up the two cats — they had been playing hide-and-seek in the rubbish — and put them back in the car, tied Jimmy to the bumper bar and settled down for the night in the car, alongside the cats, on a mattress, under a doona and still in our clothes (too cold to get completely changed).

Sleep came quickly but remarkably dawn came slowly. The first hint of light crept over the car at five-thirty and by six o'clock the dawn felt ready to hit, but instead it teased as it slowly changed from the pale yellow hue of silhouette and birdsong to the full orange and purple I had come to recognise instantly. The intensity of colour drained, fading to peach, apricot and then a shimmering white, as the full ball of sun moved over the horizon. This morning the sun wasn't on fire. It brought a cold morning, a pale, brittle blue with clouds like snow flurries strewn across the expanse of sky. For the first time on this trip it felt like winter.

One of the tyres on the car was looking flat. Jodie didn't want to drive the Tanami with a flat. In the cold morning I tried to get air into the tyre but Bruce's pump seemed to be broken. The valve wasn't sealing. Bruce didn't believe me when I told him his pump was dodgy. He lent me his 'good' pump and, as he stood next to me watching my every move, he told me that he had been out on Moola Bulla, a cattle station back up towards Halls Creek, in 1963, and then Billiluna, another station in the Kimberley, from 1964 to 1967. In 1967 he met Jacquie and bought the roadhouse. I laughed and said I was born in 1967. He smiled, that old bushman's smile, and said, 'Well, things have changed a bit in that time.'

The dog and one of the cats, Eddie, were in the car. Lucky, the white cat, flatly refused to come out from under a car wreck on the edge of the red-dirt car park. After twenty minutes of frustration, Bruce and Jodie attacked from either side and Bruce scared the cat sufficiently to make him leap into Jodie's arms.

'Good thing,' said Bruce. 'Those wild cats would have got him before too long.'

SOUTH IN THE NORTHERN TERRITORY

The road from Rabbit Flat to Yuendumu was flat, wide clay, red with sand shifting across the surface. 'Bulldust', a substance you have to be careful of because the thin film of dust hides potholes and looks deceptively stable. The earth changed colour to yellow clay and then back to red. There was a touch of green across the horizon as a result of recent rain. Rain in July?

Jodie and I joked that we were starting to drive downhill — towards Alice (or Kuminjai Springs, as Jodie called it, as do all Aboriginal people in Balgo, because someone they know called Alice died and they won't say her name again).

As we drove, the bulldust became softer, shinier, redder. The trees were taller, the scrubby grass and knee-high shrubs healthier, and there were more dead things lying on the side of the road, cattle carcasses, old cars, tyres, scattered as though by design.

The green felt odd, the desert too lush to be called a desert. There was an eagle hovering above the side of the road, so close that I could see his hook-shaped beak, sharp eyes and underbelly of brown and white.

I was drawn to that flat line of horizon again. Amazing how transfixing that pull is — always having to keep going, to move, to pass through. We overtook a cow carcass, head stuck in the mud, legs entwined in the drying red pool; it clearly couldn't get out once the rain had stopped, and the crows and eagles saw to it that it never did, its rear and stomach eaten away. A two-metre-long lizard, like a huge gecko with its chin fanned out and front legs splayed, looked crucified, flayed and desiccated, as if it had launched itself into a shrub, right on the side of the road, and died. Perhaps some humans put it there after finding such a perfect creature in death — if not, then the act of hurling itself into the shrub was one of determination and sacrifice.

But on this day, despite the variations of death everywhere, the desert didn't feel hard, didn't feel vengeful, unforgiving. There were floodways, puddles, cattle grids with green sprouting out of their sodden edges. And even though the wind retained its chill, the warmth of the sun was reflected in the runnels of bulldust and water across the corrugated road. The rain, the water, seemed to have brought hope or revival — even the red ant-made sculptures seemed fatter in the Northern Territory.

This was the kind of country I made resolutions in. So big that it reduced my life and my problems to insignificance. At the same time reinforcing the importance of everything I did, that I was a part of this story, this horizon. Possibilities for reinvention, transformation, growth seemed endless. Many things simply fell into perspective or fell away.

The traffic was increasing; we came across convoys of contractors and tourist 4WD expeditions, but Jodie beat them hands down. Gushing through the middle of the wash-outs, swinging from one side of the road to the other, avoiding the high, soft routes marked out by every other 4WD vehicle and taking the road less travelled and much more fun — red water washed over us as we screamed through the floodways — and she was the only female driver I could see as we overtook the others.

The land changed again and the MacDonnell Ranges came into view. As the clouds swirled above us I recognised this country of white ghost gums and mauve hills. It was Namatjira country. I grew up with his faded purple prints on the walls of my childhood home. Under this sky, the easy unexamined sentimentality we whiteys find when talking about the Australian desert almost makes sense.

As we drove the final leg to Alice, the land was fertile with brumbies, glossy and pregnant, in herds on the edges of the road. Calves hovered around their mothers' legs behind fences and the green folded into the rich khaki of the eucalypt trunks.

An afternoon in Alice Springs felt as though anything might happen. There was an undertow of energy that was almost tangible, a feeling, not of menace, but of strangeness. As though if you stopped and stood still and waited, all the tourists, all the business, all the busyness of the town on a Monday afternoon smack bang in the middle of the school holidays would melt away and something extraordinary would happen. As though the balloon of tourism was hiding the true nature of the place. One town. Two worlds.

I said goodbye to Jodie on a dark Alice street, and I experienced, once more, the loneliness, the intensity of remote living. We had shared something. A connection. But we both knew how different our lives were away from this, this getting from one place to another. I may never see her again in my life.

HISTORY REPEATS

Just out of Elliott into Newcastle Waters another dawn arrived over Central Australia. The sun burst across the horizon more quickly than it did at Rabbit Flat, and into a burning ball. I had to turn my head from the glare through the bus window. It was a solid-blue-sky day — and warmer — and the pink was violent in the western sky, the husky shadows of night being chased away.

The cathedrals of clay, the anthills, reappeared. Yellow rather than red, and taller, thinner than the fat doughy ones of the southern Tanami. The scrubby trees and uneven horizon of rises and mounds seemed familiar.

The anthill temples were grey at Daly Waters but very straight and lean. Perhaps they were old ones, no longer used.

A swarm of tiny finches, flashing glossy in the sun, swooped over the Brahman cattle in the paddock to the left; the cattle, with their floppy sideways ears, didn't stir. Eagles sat atop the taller trees alongside the bitumen, waiting for road kill. Black cockatoos flew by, crows bounced on the gravel beside the highway, and I was blank again, staring out the window.

I was trying to read Yann Martel's book *Self* and was stuck on the sentence that reads, 'A culture of disrespect allows for extreme moments of companionship' when I realised we were on the outskirts of Mataranka.

There was the turnoff to the thermal springs, the marker for the beginning of the town, and Willy's Autos, and the petrol station (under new ownership), the Old Elsey (under new ownership), the Stockyard Gallery (under new ownership), new houses, new shire office — the changes flew past and then the bus pulled up at the old petrol station at the far end of town. It was only a quick stop to pick up mail, so the driver didn't want his passengers to get off and I realised I was relieved. I had to come back but I wasn't ready yet.

From where I sat I could see sprinklers on the grass opposite. Picnic tables. Bougainvillea. Palms. And even on the bus I could hear the finches as they fled from an eagle that was sitting on an updraft of wind just behind them, casting shadows across the bitumen and into the green gums.

It looked like an oasis, and more beautiful than I remembered. Something the tourist brochures would make much of. When I lived here, though, it had never felt like an oasis.

OLD FRIENDS

Katherine was all hot, flat, baking light and heat. The sun was all pervasive. It really didn't feel like winter any more. The kites were keening and crying as they circled low overhead. Wide streets were filled with people moving in groups of two or three or five. Aboriginal people and white people. The bus terminal was unclean and barely functioning. I called Jack's mobile phone, left a message and made my way to the Jade Café next door, where the coffee was a nice surprise.

Jack and her daughter, Willow, her eleven-year-old whom I had never met, were bringing their Brahman cattle up from Mataranka, from their station, to exhibit them at the Katherine Show. I would be camping with them at the showgrounds, swagging it.

Jack and a young girl with short blonde hair walked in and saw me sitting at the corner table. Jack looked no different, still the thin, wiry, easy-to-humour girl I remembered from her wedding fourteen years ago. I recognised Willow instantly,

Tom written all over her face. We hugged and laughed and they helped me carry my bags to the airconditioned Toyota and then, without time for a quiet catch-up or even the niceties of 'How was your trip?' let alone 'How have the last fourteen years been?', it was all on. The Katherine Show.

The parched showgrounds, the hot and bothered cattle, the trucks, the Brahman bulls bigger than three of me. I loved it. The people; the dust; the swags; the way the stars descended as the three of us lay stretched out between hay bales under the black night sky. The early starts, with burned orange hinting around the racetrack then lifting to a light that inflicted itself on the eyes. The washing and feeding and watering of cattle. The line-ups for showers at the end of the day. Rum after dark. And the heat, the 'unseasonable' heat.

I loved getting dirty. It happened so rarely to me in the city, but here I was filthy. Dust, sweat, water, mud, cattle, caked cow shit and boozy bars. Loved it, all of it. And after nearly five days it almost killed me.

NEW OWNERSHIP

On an afternoon off from the cows, I borrowed Jack's all-terrain Toyota and drove to Mataranka. I had been feeling a little off-colour for the past 24 hours and put it down to the water at the showgrounds, but when I pulled into the Old Elsey, renamed the Mataranka Hotel 'Under New Ownership' and fell out the door of the car, I felt distinctly worse. I walked into the bar and ordered a soft drink. It was the same bar I used to work in — except for some superficial decor changes. As I lifted the soft-drink bottle to my lips, I realised I was about to throw up. I hurriedly asked if the bathrooms were in the same place; the woman behind the bar nodded and pointed, and I scampered out the side door.

Twenty-five minutes later I had divested my stomach of anything I'd eaten in the last two days, purged my bowels and just stopped crying. I could barely stand.

While I was out the back of the pub pulling myself together, I wandered about. There was our old louvred, fibro house, with much more fencing and a green shade cloth which wasn't there when I lived in the place. The old dilapidated post-and-rail fence had gone, replaced by new tourist cabins and prefab rooms with car parking spaces right where that beautiful front yard, looking east, straight across the highway, used to be. The old bougainvillea's purple flowers raged into view over the fence line but the chance to see the reflection of sunsets in the eastern sky across the highway was gone. I wondered where the lorikeets were, the ones that used to leap and twist around that dripping tap, their shots of green flashing through the dusk air.

There were more Aboriginal people in town. The old transit camp had been moved, but as I drove around the back streets and dead ends — all five of them — I realised that not much else had changed. Sure, there was the new accommodation for tourists, a new petrol station, new library and council buildings, new statues on the main strip honouring Aeneas and Jeannie Gunn, but really, the townspeople appeared as they always had. Even the woman running the servo, who had been in town for two weeks, seemed tired — and she was only in her early twenties.

I wandered past the old bowsers I used to pump petrol from, and it felt like a hundred years ago. Some kind of creeper had grown over the pumps; the pub garden had been bricked in; the wall where the 'Aboriginal window' was had been torn down to form a proper bar, and the back section was now an airconditioned pokie palace. Peter and Paula, who owned it when I worked there, had gone into receivership and a new guy had bought it. He didn't show at the pub, according to the barmaid, so 'He's a pretty good boss'.

I drove out to the thermal springs and the Homestead. It took much less time than I remembered. And the Homestead seemed bigger, covering more land than it used to. Well, the car park did, at least. I walked down the track past the bar and into the edge of the national park that leads to the springs.

There was a flood a year or so ago and the Homestead and springs were badly affected. The palm trees had been chopped down, hacked apart to clear the area up once the water receded. Where there was lush, tropical rainforest it was now grey mud and stumps. There was a new wooden ramp, a path to the springs, which elevated the tourists off the forest floor. It looked oddly out of place.

I heard the noise of the people in the springs before I saw them. It sounded like a gaggle of geese — and when I rounded the corner I realised why. There were over 200 people crammed in the pools. And the pools looked smaller than I remembered. My heart fell. This place wasn't the beautiful, tranquil piece of calm it used to be for me. It was full of tourists, and even the water itself looked unpleasant, with leaves and tree debris floating about in it. Not the clear, clean water I remembered. These springs weren't the ones I used to visit late at night with The Charmer in the dark and quiet.

I made myself get in and wade to one end of the expanse of water. The water was warm and I tried to enjoy it. I moved to a small space next to four middle-aged Australian tourists standing and chatting in the chest-high springs.

'I've known a few good ones, but you look around up here and what are they doing with the money?'

'Nothing. They don't do anything with it but drink it. I wouldn't have a drink in that town pub.'

'Well, that boy, the one back home, who trained the football team, he was good.'

'And a bloody good player.'

'And he hardly drank at all. And he even had a nice house. You know, for the street he was in.'

'These fellas just sleep out in the streets here. And they get so much money from the government.'

'But the art is beautiful — and so many galleries all along the highway. They must be making mountains of money from it, so you would think. But maybe they don't understand how to run a business … We bought a painting yesterday and bargained the guy right down.'

I ducked my head under to be able to say I went for a swim and got out.

Near the car park there was a building that was a reconstruction of Jeannie Gunn's house. She married Aeneas on 31 December 1901 in Melbourne and moved up here with him when he took on the job of managing Elsey Station. By March 1903 he was dead and Jeannie moved back to Melbourne. There she wrote her Never Never books for children — *The Little Black Princess* was my favourite — which detailed her experience of living in this remote place more than a hundred years ago. It was Jeannie Gunn who introduced me to a mythical, romantic Australia.

Standing there, looking at the rough, square replica of the Old Elsey Station house, hardly the grand place I always imagined the Gunn's lived in, and despite knowing that her books are considered patronising to indigenous people in contemporary Australia, I wondered at her bravery and character. She spent over a year living here with almost no other white people around.

She was challenged, confronted and delighted with what she found in this land, and her stories are full of the people and their lives — people who have descendants still living in the area. Romantic or not, she at least knew the ins and outs of everyday living up here.

Back in Katherine it was the Cattlemen's Association awards dinner. Willow had won lots of prizes and Jack pushed for her to get an invite. Usually there were no children allowed, as the adults want to get pissed and act up, perhaps for the one night of the year.

We all ended up going. It was held out of town at a restaurant and it was packed with girls in their good dresses and boys in tweed jackets and jeans.

The trophies were handed out at the beginning of the night and Willow took home most of the loot. Plates, trays, a light stand, trophies. The cattle had done really well, and as Willow had been the main carer for a number of them — the little bulls and heifers primarily — she got the credit. She did, however, get embarrassed with all her prizes. And then she got bored.

As the night progressed there were hands slipped under dresses, snogs at the table, a couple of guys falling over out the back and then the dancing started. The DJ was playing Yothu Yindi. The room was full of white cattle people dancing to the most famous Aboriginal band in Australia.

I found the phone in the kitchen and, after much hysterical banter with the guys washing dishes in the kitchen (two cute young gammin' guys), I finally figured out the right taxi phone number (131 008, if you ever need it) and we left just as the tone of the party was falling. Jack clearly would have liked to stay but she didn't take up my offer of looking after Willow while she partied.

Once Willow was finally asleep in her swag, Jack and I had our first real conversation since the show began. It was as though no time had slipped by. Family. Lovers. Old friends in Sydney. Schooling. Their station. Tom. How hard he worked. I mentioned The Charmer, attempting, unsuccessfully, to be offhand. Jack said he'd be around to see how the cattle did in the judging. We drank the last of the Bundaberg and Coke UDLs. We both reminded each other to buy more tomorrow.

THE SHOW

The Katherine Show was hot and dusty. Avenues of sideshows with the camp-drafting ring on one side and the main parade ring on the other. We bumped into people who remembered me from Jack's wedding fourteen years ago.

I had made a deal with Willow to go on rides with her. So, once the stock were watered and fed and a shower had, Friday was ours. First the Hurricane, a noisy Ferris wheel on its side which spun and spun faster and faster, then the Cha Cha, in quick succession. A friend of hers turned up and they headed off to do what eleven-year-old girls do together. I felt jilted.

As I wandered around the show, I realised I was expecting, waiting, for The Charmer to come the other way, to just turn up, coming round the corner. He didn't. And I hadn't called him yet. Fifteen years on I felt like the other woman all over again. I waited. But I also started to wonder if Jack had told him I was here.

I met up with Willow late in the afternoon. She had perfected the sullen almost-teenager mood. But we still hung out, me getting fed up with her and for a moment — when I swore and said 'For fuck's sake' to her — forgetting she was only eleven.

As night fell and the flashing lights of the rides and stalls took over, we got her mum and a friend onto the dodgems.

I noticed that the Aboriginal boys, the only other drivers, were wary of running into us whiteys. Me, the dumb dodgem driver that I have always been, I just screamed hysterically and ran into everyone, grinning like a loon. I caused a huge crash of cars and the boys and I fell about laughing for a second, and then we all hooned off again. The ice broken, it was on for young and old, and two of them, tiny little boys really, pointed at me, laughing, and ganged up to run me into the wall. I hadn't screamed so much in years. They should offer dodgem cars as therapy.

Then, as our turn finished and the next started, I noticed a skinny little Aboriginal girl waiting to get on a car. She was probably about ten years old and had on a pink skirt and top. On her head was a fairy-floss pink wig, slightly off-centre and not covering all of her own hair. She looked smart, street-wise. She drove like a maniac throughout her ride, pink locks flowing out behind her. Her energy was light and passionate. She was having a ball.

The last night of swagging it was sad. I didn't want to leave. I hadn't seen The Charmer. I hadn't spent enough time here. I didn't want to go back to the city. In the dark of early morning I counted four shooting stars, one after the other, arcing across the sky. The dust settled and the morning light brought a chill which soon faded into the rush of the day.

LEAVING

Willow and I scammed it so she got to drive with me in the airconditioned vehicle all the way to Darwin while her mother took the cattle truck. We listened to music and she told me about school of the air. We played Kasey Chambers and sang purposefully off key to 'Not Pretty Enough'. We cracked ourselves up. Jess, her black-and-white border collie, was leaping from side to side at the rear of the cattle truck as we followed it up the highway.

Tears and a hard, breathless panic came as I realised that I had no more opportunity to see The Charmer. The eleven-year-old didn't notice.

As we drove north, a whole procession of bikies passed us travelling south. It looked like they had a police escort. Maybe there was a bikies' get-together somewhere down the highway. I couldn't quite make out their jacket insignia — and then I did. It was the gang Kim was a member of. I couldn't believe it. There must have been at least a hundred bikies in the procession. Kim would be in there somewhere. He had probably just ridden past me.

Yet another weird coincidence; they had peppered this trip, this country, these fifteen years of my life.

Finally we hit hot, tropical Darwin. I got to my hotel in town, leaving the cattle, the eleven-year-old, Jack and Jess the dog at the Darwin showgrounds. It was a relief to be by myself for the first time in days.

The Arafura Sea threw up clouds ballooning on the horizon in a mock attempt at the wet season build-up. The heat was sexy. Darwin is a sexy town. It was almost 5 pm but it didn't feel like the end of the day, although the breeze was up and onshore. It was still 30 degrees.

Except for a cursory attempt to find the pub that Kim and his bikie mates would be drinking in if they were in town (I found it but didn't know how to leave a message for him), the next day in Darwin was relaxing — I pretended I was on holiday. The pool, the food, the heat and then dinner with Jack. Jack stayed on for more drinks. My only other friend in Darwin, a school teacher, rocked in and the three of us settled down for a bit of a session. We talked about the difficulties of schooling when you live remotely, and the teacher took issue with Jack about the only boarding school in Darwin — a school with predominantly Aboriginal students. 'I wouldn't send her there,' said Jack. I changed the subject.

We got onto The Charmer and ordered more rums. As it turned out, Jack hadn't told him I was coming up. He hadn't even known I was in town. I ordered more rum. By the time I got back to the hotel to pick up my bags to make the red-eye flight back to Sydney, I was very drunk.

DRAWING LINES IN THE SAND

Sydney was cold after the desert and Darwin. I was confused by the noise and the crowded buses. I cried down the phone to Willow when I told her I couldn't make it back for the Mataranka Rodeo to see her camp draft, cutting cattle over a designated course, for the first time. I wished I was back up there all over again.

Two weeks later, I got up enough courage to call him. I'd got his number through whitepages.com.au — strangely easy to track some people down. Fifteen years on, he was still The Charmer. Still had that warm growl in his voice, a low laugh and flat vowels. Still managed to thrill with the words 'my Pip'.

It was the same. The same as it ever was. He was still as ridiculously redneck and easily riled. And we talked about the sex. What do you do with that, the bone-cracking, earth-shattering memory of the sex? The door to desire is always there, a liminal space, and over the phone lines it was creaked open again. Ridiculous really — it had been fifteen years since we had had sex but my body responded.

The strangest thing about the conversation was that it was completely normal. It was as though we saw each other yesterday. We had dropped into each other's worlds immediately and there was no protection, no disguised vulnerability, no game.

He told me about his three children, the ones he had with his then girlfriend, now wife of many years. They sounded brilliant. And, in one of those coincidences, I had a *Sydney Morning Herald* photo of him and his son from not so long ago. 'Yes,' I said, 'that boy does look like the spitting image of you, Charm.'

I called him 'matey', and he said, 'I can't believe it — that's what you used to call me all those years ago.' We laughed. A lot. Especially when I said that these days I called everyone 'matey'.

The Charmer was running ships of livestock out of Darwin, to Indonesia and Borneo, when I last saw him. I have a beautiful letter written on his first voyage with the ship to Kota Kinabalu. It is all flat black sea and starlight and camaraderie. He had just started on the crew then but now he owns land in Bali. Owns his own station, is comfortable, some would say rich.

We talked about those times, how there hadn't been that many days that have gone past without us thinking of each other. How we agreed it was important to us both.

I told The Charmer that I had to get up enough guts to call Kim. I reminded him who Kim was, not sure if he would remember him.

I could hear The Charmer breathing in the silence that followed.

'If I ever see that bastard again he is dead.'

Right. 'Why? What happened?'

'Loads of shit. Jail. Fuckin' drugs. And he's been up on a rape charge. A mate knew the girl. He got off. Still, you're not going to call him. Ever.'

So, all these years later The Charmer was still able to floor me with his certainty and his chivalry. And perhaps I allowed his reaction, his words, to confirm my wariness of calling Kim.

He asked if I had been in contact with 'that girl, that friend of yours who didn't like me'. I knew he meant Sarah. She hadn't liked him because he was cheating on his girlfriend. But then she also had an issue with me for the same reason.

I told him that I hadn't been able to find her. I had found her children's school but no word as yet. And I hadn't been able to track down Jim.

There was another pause.

'He worked for me, your mate. On the ships. He was good.' Another pause.

'After he moved back from Queensland?'

'Yeah. He and his missus split the blanket. That one who didn't like me.'

'Yep. They did. They split the blanket.'

'He worked for me for a while. And then he got sick. He got gut rot. He was real sick. He died, Pip, he died. A few years after you left. He wasn't even old.'

Jim was dead. I wasn't sure if I was hearing right. 'Bowel cancer, mate. He died drinking soup.'

Jim was dead.

The phone call lasted two hours. Two hours of laughter and tears. Two hours later and I knew that Kim was a renegade, a criminal, Jim was dead and The Charmer hadn't changed. The three men who were so important to me all those years ago wound up bound together.

I think again about contacting Kim. I will, but I am not sure when.